A History of Mt. Mitchell
and the Black Mountains

Exploration, Development, and Preservation

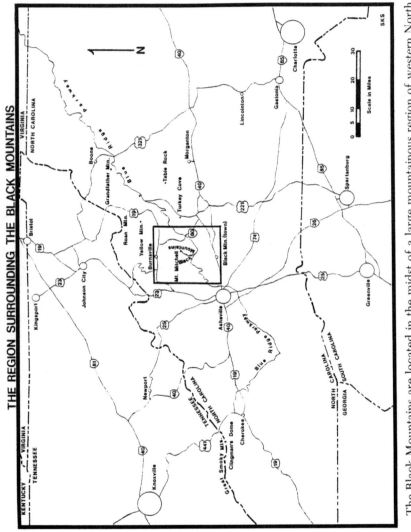

THE REGION SURROUNDING THE BLACK MOUNTAINS

The Black Mountains are located in the midst of a large mountainous region of western North Carolina. The blocked-off area in the center of the map is shown enlarged on the opposite page. Map prepared by the author.

THE BLACK MOUNTAINS

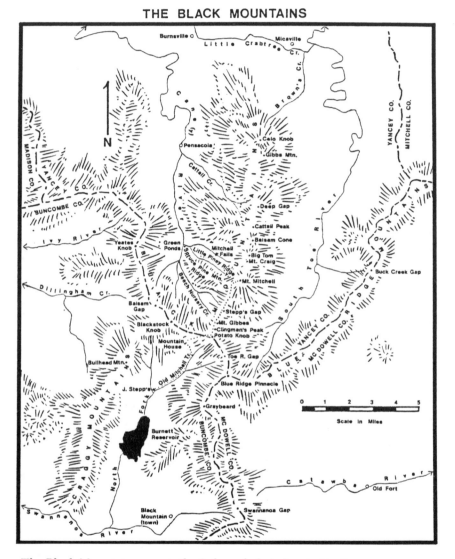

The Black Mountain range is the *J*-shaped chain located in the top-center portion of the map. The Blue Ridge range to the east separates the waters that flow into the Atlantic Ocean from those that flow into the Gulf of Mexico. Map prepared by the author.

A History of Mt. Mitchell
and the Black Mountains
Exploration, Development, and Preservation

S. Kent Schwarzkopf

Raleigh

Division of Archives and History
North Carolina Department of Cultural Resources

Division of Parks and Recreation
North Carolina Department of Natural Resources
and Community Development

1985

Third Printing, 1994

Contents

Illustrations

Foreword

Interest in the history of western North Carolina has grown appreciably in recent years. County histories, specialized studies on Appalachian life and culture, and continuing fascination with the Cherokee presence have all attracted public and scholarly attention. In publishing this first comprehensive history of Mt. Mitchell and the Black Mountains, the Historical Publications Section of the North Carolina Division of Archives and History hopes to contribute a significant chapter to the understanding of and historical literature on western North Carolina.

The Black Mountain range rises more than 6,000 feet above sea level and contains the highest peaks in the eastern United States. From its earliest recorded history the range attracted the interest of such prominent scientists as André Michaux, Moses Ashley Curtis, Elisha Mitchell, and Arnold Guyot. During the late antebellum period tourists discovered the scenic beauty of the region, and William Patton's Mountain House became the departure point for excursions through rugged elevations. It was also during the 1850s that the Black Mountains were the subject of a controversy of major proportions between Elisha Mitchell, science professor at the University of North Carolina, and United States Congressman Thomas L. Clingman. Clingman accurately identified the highest peak of the Black Mountain range in 1855 and, in so doing, cast doubt on Mitchell's prior claim to having ascended the highest mountain in the 1830s or 1840s. Mitchell's tragic death in 1857 brought an abrupt end to his participation in the controversy, but his burial on the high peak the following year assured that his name would be permanently attached to the mountain. In a fitting memorial Mt. Mitchell State Park became North Carolina's first state park in 1915.

S. Kent Schwarzkopf, a native of Asheville, began this study of Mt. Mitchell and the Black Mountains as an employee of the Division of Parks and Recreation in the North Carolina Department of Natural Resources and Community Development during the mid-1970s. He produced a meticulously researched 400-page manuscript that served as the parent document for the first half of the present work. He continued working on the history of Mt. Mitchell as a graduate student at Oregon State University in Corvallis, Oregon, from which he holds master's degrees in history and geography. Mr. Schwarzkopf has worked as a naturalist and historian for the National Park Service at such sites as Sequoia National Park, California; Crater Lake National

Park, Oregon; Rocky Mountain National Park, Colorado; and the Blue Ridge Parkway, North Carolina.

The Division of Archives and History wishes to thank the Division of Parks and Recreation for permission to publish Mr. Schwarzkopf's history of the Black Mountains. The cooperation of James S. Stevens, Jr., former director of Parks and Recreation, and Kirk Fuller, former state parks historian, is especially appreciated.

Robert M. Topkins edited the manuscript and saw it through press. Stephena K. Williams prepared the manuscript on a word processor for typesetting, and Sally A. Copenhaver assisted with the proof-reading.

Jeffrey J. Crow
Historical Publications Administrator

August 1994

Preface

The Black Mountain range, a part of the southern Appalachians, rises above fertile mountain valleys thirty miles northeast of Asheville, North Carolina. For most of its length, the range reaches an elevation exceeding 6,000 feet. Because of the relatively even elevation of its ridgeline, the range was referred to as a single mountain until the late 1850s. Of the separate peaks that have since been designated, six are among the ten highest in the eastern United States.

Although the Black Mountain range is the highest in the eastern United States, its length and breadth do not equal that of the nearby Blue Ridge or Great Smoky mountains. From the air, the range bears the shape of the letter *J*, and the distance between its end points— Yeates Knob and Celo Knob—is but fifteen miles. The valley enclosed by the *J* is that of the Cane River and its tributaries. To the west, the range is drained by the Ivy River; to the south, by the North Fork of the Swannanoa River; and to the east, by the South Toe River. Since the Black Mountains lie to the west of the Blue Ridge (the eastern continental divide), all the streams that flow from its slopes eventually reach the Gulf of Mexico.

The highest peak in the range, and the highest point east of the Mississippi River, is Mt. Mitchell, a mountain whose name is better known than that of the range itself. The mountain, with an elevation of 6,684 feet, is named in honor of Elisha Mitchell, one of a number of prominent scientists who explored and studied the range's towering heights. Mitchell, because of the popular appeal of his mountain-measuring work, a controversy in which he engaged with United States Congressman Thomas L. Clingman, and the unusual circumstances of his death, is the best-known, if not the most significant, personality in the history of the range.

Antedating the mountain-measuring work of Mitchell and others were explorations of the range's flora made by prominent botanists. The Black Mountains rise 3,500 to 4,000 feet above the valley floors, and a wide variety of plants are found on their slopes. Three forest zones are present: an oak-hickory forest at the lower elevations, a northern deciduous forest from about 4,500 to 5,500 feet above sea level, and a spruce-fir forest at the highest elevations. Probably more than fifty types of trees and a thousand species of flowering plants can be found in the range. Of particular interest is the paper birch. Separated by more than 800 miles from the northern variety of paper birch, these trees can be found within a relatively narrow elevation band of a portion of the Black Mountains.

Like the flora, the fauna of this nationally recognized natural landmark is abundant and diverse. Among large mammals, the Virginia white-tailed deer is most often seen; but the black bear is also present. Bobcats and even mountain lions are seen on rare occasions. Among the smaller mammals, the woodchuck and the red squirrel are abundant at the higher elevations. The cool temperatures of the high elevations make it very unlikely that one would encounter snakes; however, these cool temperatures, along with abundant precipitation, make the range a haven for salamanders.

By any account, the Black Mountains are very old. Geologically, the mountains are made of ancient pre-Cambrian igneous and metamorphic rocks that are believed by scientists to have been formed before life inhabited the land. Millions of years ago the Black Mountains stood loftier and more rugged, perhaps much like the younger Rocky Mountains of the western United States. But—over time—wind, water, and other forces have worn the range to its more subdued yet enduring present profile.

While the Black Mountains have witnessed the passage of great geologic time, they have also had a long and rich human history. For more than 200 years the natural beauty and diversity of the range have attracted scientists and tourists from throughout the eastern United States. More recently, during the early twentieth century, the denuding of the range's forests sparked one of the first preservation efforts in the eastern United States. The following pages will provide a closer look at the personalities and events that have helped shape the human history of the Black Mountains. From early scientific explorers and settlers to tourists and lumbermen, humankind has left its mark on the Black Mountains—the highest mountains in the eastern United States.

Acknowledgments

The author's foremost appreciation is extended to: Clifford H. Phillips, for initiating the author's research into the history of the Black Mountains and providing subsequent support; to Boyd Mattison and Mark Simpson, for their provoking dialogue and leads to dozens of research sources on scientific exploration and logging operations in the Black Mountains; and to Betty Lawrence, for her continuous encouragement and research assistance. Thanks is also extended to the following individuals who gave of their time and knowledge in providing research assistance: Philip Banks, Whitfield J. Bell, Lewis Buck, Selden Cooper, Alice Cotten, Jerry Cotten, Garland Draper, Jim Flatness, Guy Gosselin, Edith Holmes, Lewis R. Ledford, Ruth E. McGuyre, Richard Schrader, Ralph H. Schwarzkopf, Evelyn Sutton, Deborah Jean Warner, and John T. Wood. For reviewing various stages of the author's work on the history of the Mt. Mitchell area, the advice of the following individuals is gratefully acknowledged: Perry Brown, Rudy Camblos, Alice Cotten, Terrell Crow, Juanita Eller, Michael Freed, Royal Jackson, Harley Jolley, Thomas McClintock, and David Shafer. Thomas Kloster assisted the author in the preparation of the large-scale map of the Black Mountains. Finally, the North Carolina Division of Parks and Recreation is thanked for the financial assistance it provided for much of the author's research on the Black Mountains.

I

Initial Habitation of the Area Surrounding the Black Mountains: Native American and White

Long before explorers and settlers left Europe in search of the New World, various Indian tribes inhabited the Black Mountain region of what is now western North Carolina. Anthropologists refer to the Indians who lived there as "Eastern Woodland" cultures. Although present knowledge of the Eastern Woodland cultures is far from complete, it is thought that they may have inhabited the area as early as 15,000 years ago.

Considerable information has been gleaned from an archaeological site located on the campus of Warren Wilson College ten miles east of Asheville and ten miles south of the southern end of the Black Mountains. Anthropologists have discovered at this site evidence of cultures dating as far back as 5,000 B.C. One of these cultures, the Pisgah, is believed to be a predecessor of the modern Cherokee. The Pisgah culture existed at the site from about A.D. 1000 to 1400, and at its height the village consisted of about a dozen houses. Archaeological evidence indicates that the Indians who inhabited this site were primarily hunters, fishermen, and plant gatherers, although they also are known to have cultivated maize, squash, and beans.

By the time the first white explorers and traders began to enter the Black Mountain region in the seventeenth century, the Cherokee Nation had become well established in the southern Appalachians. Its population is estimated to have been 22,000, making it one of the largest tribes in the United States. The Cherokee homeland was centered in western North Carolina, eastern Tennessee, northeastern Georgia, and northwestern South Carolina. In western North Carolina, the Cherokee lived predominantly in settlements along the Tuckasegee, Little Tennessee, and Valley rivers, all located to the west of the Black Mountains. Their hunting territory, however, did include the Black Mountain range and even extended eastward into the upper piedmont region.

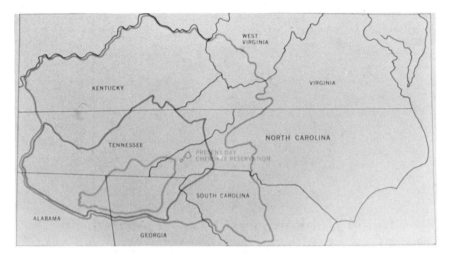

The Black Mountains were included as part of the land claimed by the Cherokee, but the principal Cherokee settlements were all west of Asheville. Through a series of treaties, the Cherokee boundary was gradually pushed westward in response to expanding white settlement. Map courtesy Great Smoky Mountains National Park, Gatlinburg, Tennessee.

The Cherokee, no doubt, traveled in the vicinity of the Black Mountains to hunt, trade, gather plants, and make war against neighboring tribes. An important Indian trail that crossed the Blue Ridge Mountains at Swannanoa Gap was known by the Cherokee name *Suwa'li-nunna' (-hi)* or Suwali Trail. The route of this trail has long served as a major access from North Carolina's piedmont to its mountains, a route closely followed at the present time by Interstate Highway 40.

The Cherokee presence north and east of the Black Mountains manifests itself in the name of the Toe River. The name "Toe" is a contraction of the Cherokee *Estatoe*, which, according to tradition, was the name of a beautiful Indian princess who lived somewhere in the Toe River valley. Legend has it that Estatoe fell in love with a tribal enemy who was killed while canoeing her away from her people. The distraught Estatoe could not endure the grief and guilt, and she drowned herself in the river that now bears her name.

The fact that the Cherokee made their camps and settlements in the river valleys does not mean that they did not, at least occasionally, ascend to the higher elevations of the region. Indeed, the Cherokee, like most Indian tribes, often preferred to travel mountain ridges both for safety (enemy tribes could be better seen) and for avoiding river and stream crossings.

2

While an abundance of game animals in the valleys and lower slopes spared the Cherokee the necessity of hunting in the higher mountains, the tribe is known to have collected from the higher elevations some of the more than five hundred plant species that they used for medicine, food, or dye. Among the plants collected by the Cherokee, some—such as Fraser's fir, red spruce, gooseberry, red raspberry, and white alder—can be found only above elevations of 4,000 or 5,000 feet. Fraser's fir, or balsam, as it is more commonly called, seems to have been a panacea for the Cherokee inasmuch as it was used for such diverse ailments as lung pains, kidney trouble, internal ulcers, colds, venereal diseases, and constipation. The plant's resin also served as a seasoner for other medicines, and it was said to be highly effective when used externally on fresh wounds.

Several Cherokee spirits—among them the eagle, the raven, and frost—were thought to dwell in the high mountains. Because the Cherokee are known to have engaged in special magical rites or "conjuring" in high mountain gaps, their belief in such spirits does not appear to have prevented them from venturing to the higher elevations. Whether or not the Cherokee or any other Indians reached any of the high peaks of the Black Mountains prior to the arrival of the white man is pure speculation. Evidence that the Cherokee used ridgetop trails, utilized plants found only at high elevations, and engaged in religious conjuring in the high gaps makes it entirely possible that Indians were the first people to reach the crest of the Black Mountains.

The Indian occupation of the Black Mountain area was not to endure. During the late 1700s and early 1800s the advancing tide of American settlement brought a dramatic change to North Carolina's mountain region. Contact between the Cherokee and the white man did not occur suddenly, however. For nearly a century before the arrival of settlers in the southern Appalachians, white men had traded with the Cherokee.

For most of the eighteenth century, traders entering the mountains came primarily from South Carolina. Early in that century the South Carolina colonial government had begun to license individual traders and regulate their trade with the Cherokee. Interestingly, North Carolina never exhibited much interest in the Cherokee trade; and while Virginia and Georgia were interested, they could do little to loosen the grip South Carolina had acquired. The traders lived among the Indians and often intermarried with them. In exchange for deerskins and furs, the traders gave the Cherokee such diverse items as guns, blankets, salt, bracelets, mirrors, and rum. The Cherokee trade was no small operation; even by 1708, 50,000 skins, valued at approximately £2,500 to £3,000, were being exported annually from the colony of South Carolina.

At first the Indian trade was highly satisfactory to both the white man and the Cherokee, and relations between the two peoples were peaceful. By the 1730s, however, this relationship had become increasingly strained. The moral character of the white men who traded with the Indians began to deteriorate, and by the 1760s, when white settlers began to enter the region, the Cherokee-white relationship was very poor.

Many of the white settlers came for different purposes and shared values quite different from those of the traders. They often had families with them, and their desire for a new life and new land came into direct conflict with the Cherokee. With the relatively peaceful conditions established at the end of the French and Indian War, white settlers began to enter the southern Appalachian territory of the Cherokee. To mollify concern among the Indians and regulate settlement, the British government in 1763 established a line at the crest of the Blue Ridge Mountains beyond which no settlers were to pass; but in the absence of strict enforcement, such a deterrent did little to suppress the westward push of American settlement. Within a short time, settlers were moving into the present states of Tennessee and Kentucky.

By 1760 settlement in North Carolina had advanced only as far as the western piedmont, and it was not until the 1770s that a sizable number of North Carolinians crossed the Blue Ridge. Because western North Carolina was more mountainous and contained numerous Cherokee settlements, would-be settlers who moved from the North Carolina piedmont generally avoided the North Carolina mountains and instead followed a northwestward course into the present states of Tennessee and Kentucky. Prospective settlers heading southwestward from Pennsylvania joined those from the North Carolina piedmont in making the eastern Tennessee valleys of the Watauga, Holston, and Nolichucky rivers the first areas of considerable settlement in the southern Appalachian region. As a result of the influx into this area, seven counties (presently in Tennessee)—Washington, Sullivan, Greene, Davidson, Sumner, Hawkins, and Tennessee—were formed between 1777 and 1788. Some of the immigration extended into present-day Watauga County, North Carolina. In 1775 migration into Kentucky was spurred by the promotional efforts of Richard Henderson (1735-1785), a North Carolina lawyer and judge, and Daniel Boone (1734-1820), a hunter, trapper, and explorer from northwestern North Carolina. Like Tennessee, Kentucky grew rapidly, and it became a state in 1792—just one year after North Carolina's first county entirely west of the Blue Ridge (Buncombe) had come into existence.

Because of the Cherokee presence in western North Carolina, settlement of the area conformed more closely with the boundaries established in white men's treaties with the Cherokee. A treaty signed in 1777 at the conclusion of hostilities between the Cherokee and white men from Virginia and the Carolinas delineated the western boundary of settlement along a line that followed the Black Mountain range from Yeates Knob to Potato Knob; this treaty officially opened the valleys of the Cane and Toe rivers to settlement. Eight years later, in 1785, the valley of the Swannanoa River was opened to settlement and the boundary line with the Cherokee Nation was extended approximately to present-day Asheville. As the white population grew, the settlement boundary continued to be pushed further westward by a series of treaties. The final blow to the Cherokee came in 1838 and 1839 when the United States government forcibly removed them from their southern Appalachian homeland to new territory that the government had provided for them in the Oklahoma Territory. This removal, an oft-told story of death and misery, became known as the "Trail of Tears." Of the approximately 17,000 Cherokee who followed the Trail of Tears, about one third died along the way from exposure or exhaustion. About 1,000 Cherokee escaped the removal by hiding out in the Great Smoky Mountains and other nearby ranges. They later became known as the Eastern

The United States government forcibly removed the Cherokee from their cabins in the southern Appalachians to land set aside in present-day Oklahoma. Because thousands of Cherokee perished during the course of the journey, it became known as the "Trail of Tears." Photograph courtesy Great Smoky Mountains National Park.

Band of Cherokee Indians, and they obtained two small reservations south of the Great Smokies on which to reside.

A few pioneers settled in that portion of North Carolina just west of the Blue Ridge prior to the time it was officially opened to settlement. To the south of the Black Mountains, Samuel Davidson crossed the Blue Ridge in 1784 by way of Swannanoa Gap; there he sought to establish a farmstead in the Swannanoa valley midway between the present-day communities of Oteen and Swannanoa. Although an Indian ambush soon put an end to Davidson's plans, other settlers arrived within the next few years to give permanence to white settlement in the lower Swannanoa valley. By 1791 the presence of whites had become substantial enough to justify the creation of Buncombe County. During the 1790s, if not before, additional settlement occurred along the expansive French Broad River valley and some of its tributaries. The valley of the Ivy River, at the western base of Yeates Knob, became home to Solomon Brigman, John Ogle, and other early settlers. By the first decade of the nineteenth century, Frederick Burnet and others had entered the valley of the North Fork of the Swannanoa. Buncombe County's population grew rapidly during the early 1800s, and by 1830 the county could claim more than 16,000 inhabitants. Asheville, situated near the confluence of the Swannanoa and French Broad rivers, was incorporated as Buncombe's county seat in 1797.

The Cane and Toe river valleys to the north and east of the Black Mountains were settled at approximately the same time as the Buncombe County valleys. However, unlike the Buncombe valleys, which were settled primarily from the east, the valleys of the Cane and Toe attracted many settlers from the north who passed over the boundary from Tennessee into North Carolina. The number of settlers coming into the area of present-day Avery, Mitchell, and Yancey counties during the 1780s was such that by 1790 more than 500 inhabitants resided in the region. John Edwards, James Hensley, Holland Higgins, and Thomas Ray were among the first to take up residence in the Cane River valley, probably in its lower or middle reaches. The upper (more southerly) portion of the Cane River valley and the South Toe valley were settled somewhat later. In 1833 Yancey County was formed from parts of Buncombe and Burke counties. Its county seat, Burnsville, was established the following year. The county grew at a much slower rate than Buncombe, a phenomenon undoubtedly influenced by the fact that its major valleys were narrower and situated at higher elevations than those in Buncombe County.

A large majority of the early settlers who entered Buncombe and Yancey counties were of Scotch-Irish or English extraction. Most

6

In order to erect cabins and secure farmland, early settlers were obliged to clear the densely vegetated southern Appalachian forests. Outbuildings such as corn cribs or smokehouses were added later. Engraving from "A Winter in the South," Part 3, *Harper's New Monthly Magazine*, XV (November, 1857), p. 734.

were young people of limited means who were looking for a more independent life in a new land—a land that was not yet settled and where prospects for game were good. Their dwellings were often windowless one-room log cabins. Like the Indians, the white settlers tended to occupy the bottomlands of the rivers, where the soil was rich and deep. They were largely self-sufficient, consuming what they farmed and hunted. Members of each household customarily made their own clothing and tanned their own leather. Families were generally large. In the spirit of cooperation, different families would get together to plant, cultivate, and harvest their crops. House-raisings, log-rollings, and cornhuskings provided additional economic and social benefits.

Agriculture was the predominant occupation of Buncombe and Yancey county inhabitants during the nineteenth century. In the mid-1800s corn and oats were the major crops, with wheat, rye, potatoes, tobacco, flax, fruit, and hay being produced in smaller quantities. Because land was relatively abundant and its price so cheap (25 to 50 cents per acre in the mid-1840s), farmers would simply move onto a

Atop some of the high ridges of the Black Mountains, open meadows, or "prairies," as they were called in the nineteenth century, provided pasturage for sheep, cattle, or swine during the warm season. Photograph (ca. 1907) courtesy North Carolina Collection, Pack Memorial Public Library, Asheville.

new piece of land when the land on which they had been working became unproductive.

The raising of livestock was also important in the vicinity of the Black Mountains. In 1850 Yancey County could claim 29,000 swine, 20,000 sheep, and 10,000 head of cattle. Not only did the region's valleys receive use as pasturage, but the slopes and summits of its mountains were likewise utilized for that purpose. Indeed, high-elevation grazing had begun by 1810. In that year John Ogle was living at least temporarily at an elevation of more than 5,000 feet just north of the Black Mountains. Ogle, who about 1795 had settled in the Ivy River valley, became active in the affairs of Buncombe County and served for a time as assistant sheriff. Sometime between 1795 and 1810 he built a house and "improvements" on a relatively flat portion of the ridgeline dividing Buncombe and Yancey counties three miles north of Yeates Knob. This may well have been the earliest habitation to be built above 5,000 feet anywhere in the eastern United States. The open, meadowlike area, which early maps and documents referred to as "Ogle's improvement," is known as Ogle Meadows at the present time. Although it is not known whether Ogle's improvement was used for grazing, such use seems likely in

8

light of its location in an area too elevated to support the growth of crops and impractical at that time as a site for logging operations. The fact that the grassy summits of two higher southern Appalachian mountains (Roan Mountain, North Carolina/Tennessee, and White-top Mountain, Virginia) were being used for pasturage in the 1820s and 1830s further supports the likelihood of such use at Ogle Meadows.

By the 1850s, if not before, the higher elevations of the Black Mountains themselves were being used for grazing. One such area was at Black Mountain Gap, where present-day N.C. Highway 128 joins the Blue Ridge Parkway. Private land was considered free range at the time, and a number of families likely used the Black Mountains to graze their few head of cattle or other livestock. The livestock were driven in the early spring from the valleys to the mountains, where they were allowed to fatten themselves on the lush vegetation until the arrival of cold weather six or seven months later.

The settlers also made use of the natural bounty of the land. Like the Cherokee before them, white nineteenth-century mountain inhabitants gathered native plants for their medicinal value. They collected ginseng, bloodroot, snakeroot, sassafras, dogwood, balsam, helle-bore, mayapple, partridge berry, raspberry, and other plants during the early and mid-1800s. The most valuable of these was ginseng, or "sang," as it was called by the mountaineers. Ginseng roots were collected primarily to be sold to the Chinese, who held the plant in especially high regard for its alleged medicinal and aphrodisiac qualities. The plant was in such demand in the early and mid-nineteenth century that during a single year a Burnsville merchant obtained from local inhabitants 86,000 pounds of ginseng root worth approximately $10,300. Such rampant collection of a plant that had never been particularly abundant nearly resulted in its decimation by about 1870. The ginseng plant was able to maintain itself, however, and it is estimated that at the present time 6,000 to 8,000 pounds of ginseng are collected annually in western North Carolina.

Only one plant collected by the early inhabitants of the Black Mountain region was strictly limited to the higher elevations: Fraser's fir or balsam. Like the Indians, the early settlers collected the resin of the balsam for its ability to heal both external injuries and internal disorders. Balsam resin was collected by pricking the resin-containing blisters with a knife and directing the resin into a collecting vial by means of an open turkey quill. In 1828 Elisha Mitchell (1793-1857), longtime professor of chemistry, mineralogy, and geology at the University of North Carolina, noted that local inhabitants were collecting balsam resin in the area of Grandfather Mountain (in present-day Avery County), and it appears that it was being gathered on the upper slopes of the Black Mountains by the 1830s.

9

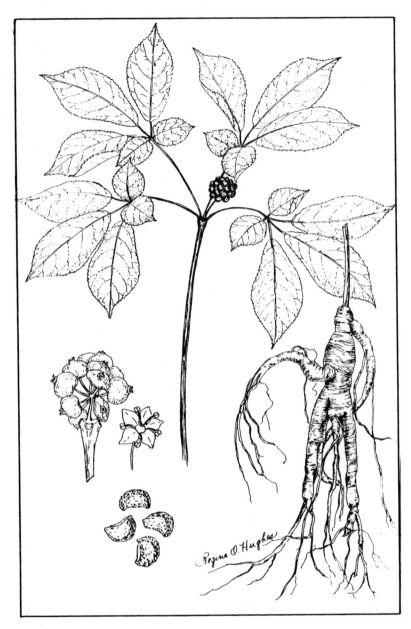

Ginseng, a relatively rare plant, has been collected by mountain inhabitants since the late 1700s. It was sold to the Chinese for its alleged medicinal and aphrodisiac qualities. Drawing by Regina O. Hughes; reproduced courtesy United States Department of Agriculture.

The Appalachian hunter probably sought the black bear more than any other animal. Photograph from the files of Mt. Mitchell State Park.

Early settlers also utilized the native wildlife of the southern Appalachians, both for their own sustenance and for trade. It seems that no animal was used to a greater extent than the bear. The bear's meat was highly prized as a source of food; its fat provided the settler with a source of grease and oil; and its skin was a valuable trade commodity, with good ones selling for $1.50 to $2.00 each during the first decade of the nineteenth century. In addition to bear, other mammals such as deer, otter, mink, red or black fox, raccoon, and muskrat were used in the fur trade.

An abundant supply of game animals remained in the valleys surrounding the Black Mountains during the early years of settlement. Only an increase in settlement would have caused a local inhabitant to ascend to the higher elevations of the range in search of game. By the 1850s such pressure from increased population was evident. Settlement extended to the upper ends of both the Cane River and North Fork valleys, and the latter valley—just seven miles in length— had acquired a population of about 250 people. But even during the 1830s a considerable degree of hunting was occurring at the middle and upper elevations of the Black Mountains. One North Fork settler, Frederic Burnett (son of Frederick Burnet, who had earlier settled the valley), even made the remarkable claim of having killed more than 600 bears prior to 1850. Such extensive hunting, engaged in for sustenance, for economic gain, and for protection of the settler's livestock, nearly resulted in the extirpation of a number of wildlife species by the time of the Civil War.

Transportation in the mountains of western North Carolina developed slowly in comparison to the piedmont and coastal plain regions of the state. The mountains not only isolated western North Carolina from the rest of the state but also contributed to differences in rates of development within the mountain region. In Buncombe County, with its relatively long and broad valleys, roads could be constructed with comparably little difficulty. Probably the first wagon road in Buncombe was the east-west route that followed the old Suwali Trail through Swannanoa Gap. The Buncombe Turnpike, a north-south road that opened in 1827, was said to be the finest road in North Carolina at the time. Yancey County was not so fortunate, and the few roads that did pass through the county in the 1830s were in much need of improvement.

During the first three decades of the nineteenth century, Asheville and Morganton were the closest trading communities for settlers living in the valleys surrounding the Black Mountains. Even so, a journey to either town took at least a full day for many inhabitants. Morganton, in the western piedmont, was the first to be settled; and at the beginning of the nineteenth century it contained about fifty wooden houses, primarily owned by tradesmen. Inhabitants living in the vicinity of the Black Mountains journeyed to Asheville or Morganton to trade dried hams, bacon, bear- or deerskins, ginseng, dried fruit, butter, or tallow for such items as salt, sugar, coffee, or molasses. When livestock needed to be sold off, mountain families sometimes pooled their resources in order to make the lengthy trip to a large trading center such as Charleston, South Carolina, or Saltville, Virginia.

The Black Mountains did not impede travel among the major valley systems of the Catawba, French Broad, and Swannanoa rivers. They did, however, form a barrier between the valleys of Buncombe and those of Yancey. Even within Yancey County, the valleys of the upper Cane and South Toe rivers were isolated from one another. To a lesser degree, the isolation of these Yancey County valleys still exists at the present time.

Perhaps because of its rural character, North Carolina, particularly its isolated mountain region, was slow to support public education. Prior to passage of a state public school law in 1839, the only education to be found below the university level was in private academies, which were often church affiliated or controlled. Newton Academy, established in Asheville prior to 1793, and Burnsville Academy, founded in 1845, achieved distinction in the Black Mountain region. Buncombe County approved a public school program in 1839, and Yancey County did so several years later. Only about half of school-aged children attended the two- to three-month annual sessions. Although illiteracy was apparently widespread throughout North Carolina during the early 1800s, the percentage of adult white illiterates in Buncombe and Yancey counties decreased to about 15 percent by 1850.

Religion was a strong and controlling influence in the lives of some early settlers. Although denominational membership was at first small, the Great Revival, a series of groundswells of renewed interest in religion, swept over North Carolina periodically from about 1800 to 1860 and bolstered church influence and membership among the common people. The Baptists, with their simple form of service and emphasis on revivals and emotional religion, became the major denomination of the early inhabitants of Buncombe and Yancey counties. The Methodists, with their aggressive evangelism, use of circuit riders, and emphasis on camp meetings and humanitarianism, were a close second. Gibbs Mountain, at the northeastern end of the Black Mountains, was probably named for William J. Gibbs, a nineteenth-century Methodist circuit rider who resided in the South Toe valley. Because of the shortage of pastors and lengthy traveling distances, religious services during the early and mid-nineteenth century could be held only infrequently at individual churches.

To these early white inhabitants, and to the Indians that preceded them, the Black Mountain region was home. Their relationship to the mountains towering above them was an intimate one. Yet, their presence did little to make known the existence and significance of the range. Such developments awaited the arrival of scientific explorers in the region.

II

The Earliest Scientific Explorations:
In Search of New Plants

About the time settlers were first entering western North Carolina, men with a very different purpose were traveling into the region. These men were botanists and plant collectors, and their presence aroused both interest and puzzlement among the settlers. While traveling in the mountains in 1839, Moses Ashley Curtis (1808-1872), a botanist and minister from eastern North Carolina, commented:

> Our appearance on the road, with our Portfolios swung over our backs . . . excites great curiosity, & we are sometimes teased out of patience by people who cannot be made to understand our business. They cannot comprehend the reason or the sense of so much labor & toil, where no money is to be made. . . . In the Mts. they think we want the plants . . . for Thomsonian practice.[1]

Curtis was attracted to the state's mountain region both by the desire to add to the world's knowledge of botany and the need to "invigorate my constitution." He was preceded, however, by botanists and plant collectors who entered western North Carolina as early as the 1770s.

Many of these early plantsmen were motivated by science, but they were, of necessity, also concerned with finding plants whose beauty or economic value would provide them financial support. In light of the great variety of plants that grow in the southern Appalachians, the early botanists had little difficulty in finding a suitable selection. They collected rhododendrons, azaleas, and magnolias destined for some of Europe's finest gardens. As for plants of economic value, the abundant oaks of the southern Appalachians proved to be particularly useful for naval construction. The botanists and plant collectors had other motives, too, such as the desire to explore and travel and to achieve a sort of immortality that the discovery of new species of plants would give them.

14

Moses Ashley Curtis (1808-1872) was among a second generation of botanists to explore the Black Mountains. A native of Massachusetts, Curtis spent most of his adult life in North Carolina as an Episcopal minister and investigator of the state's natural history. Engraving from *Journal of the Elisha Mitchell Scientific Society for the Year 1884-1885* (Raleigh: Edwards, Broughton and Co., 1885), frontispiece.

During the early and mid-1700s naturalists Mark Catesby (1679?-1749) and John Bartram (1699-1777) became the first plantsmen to reach the foothills of the southern Appalachians. In 1776 Bartram's son, William (1739-1823), penetrated the mountain region by entering the Cherokee country of North Carolina to the west of Asheville. Not until the latter part of the eighteenth century, however, did botanical exploration in the southern Appalachians increase to the extent that the Black Mountains and other mountain groups in western North Carolina received their first serious attention in the name of science.

The man most instrumental in this more widespread botanical exploration was André Michaux, a French botanist who became the first white man known to have set foot in the Black Mountains. Michaux (1746-1802) was a farmer in his early life, but during his mid-twenties he became interested in plants and exploration. Michaux's travels took him to many parts of the world—to Persia, Madagascar, Hudson Bay, and the United States. In 1785 Michaux found the French government quite interested in introducing into its royal plantations the most valuable trees of eastern North America; this provided him with his first opportunity to visit the United States.

Accompanied by his only son, Francois André, then fifteen years old, Michaux arrived in New York in October, 1785. In 1787, after several brief botanical excursions into New Jersey, Pennsylvania, and Maryland, Michaux headed south to the warmer climate of the Carolinas. About ten miles from Charleston he established a nursery, which was to remain his headquarters until he left America nine years later. Michaux wasted little time in heading for the mountains of North Carolina, which he undoubtedly had heard mentioned by William Bartram, with whom he was acquainted. In the spring of 1787 and again in the autumn of 1788 Michaux followed the valley of the Savannah River and explored its headwaters near the point at which the present boundaries of North Carolina, South Carolina, and Georgia meet.

In 1789 Michaux journeyed further into the mountainous region of North Carolina. It was during this trip that he became the first white man known to have ascended the Black Mountains. Leaving Charleston in early June, 1789, Michaux traveled by way of Camden, Charlotte, and Lincolnton and arrived at "Burke court house" (Morganton) on June 13. He stopped at the plantation of Colonel Waightstill Avery near Morganton and continued on to the home of a Captain Ainsworth in Turkey Cove, a picturesque lowland near the present-day junction of N.C. Highway 226 and U.S. Highway 221. This was apparently the last habitation Michaux saw before beginning his ascent of the Black Mountains, about twenty-five miles away. Perhaps accompanied by Ainsworth, Michaux left for the range on June 17 and returned to Turkey Cove six days later. Considering the distance involved, he probably spent only two or three days collecting plants and exploring in the Black Mountains. Regrettably, his diary is incomplete concerning the trip. Although Michaux noted that he

Viburnum alnifolium or hobblebush is the showiest of several species of viburnums André Michaux may have seen during his June, 1789, ascent of the Black Mountains. Photograph (1979) by the author.

16

found a few new species of blueberries, azaleas, and viburnum, the mention of these plants gives no indication of the elevation to which he ascended. This, combined with the absence of any locational information, makes the route of Michaux's first visit to the Black Mountains uncertain. After his excursion to the Black Mountains, Michaux passed over Yellow Mountain (in present-day Avery County) on his way to Tennessee and Virginia and eventually made his way back to Charleston.

Michaux must have been impressed with the Black Mountains, for in November, 1789, just two months after he had returned to Charleston, he once again set out for the North Carolina mountains. He followed the same route that he had taken in June and arrived at Turkey Cove on November 20. On the twenty-third he set out for the "hautes Montagnes" (high mountains), and the following day he crossed the Blue Ridge. On November 25 he arrived at the "parties basses de la Montagne Noire" (the lower portions of the Black Mountain). On that and the following day Michaux collected on the slopes of the Black Mountains sharp-leaved magnolia, Fraser's magnolia, two types of azalea, and a number of other plants that he did not specifically mention. There is some evidence that Michaux's exploration of the mountain range transpired on the eastern slopes above the South Toe River inasmuch as he noted that he passed by some waterfalls on the "Taw river" prior to returning to Turkey Cove. No indication is given that Michaux ascended to the crest of the range, which likely would have been a chilling prospect at that time of year. Michaux spent five days botanizing the mountains in the vicinity of Turkey Cove; and when he packed up his collection, he had some 2,500 specimens of trees, shrubs, and other plants to show for his efforts.

During the next few years Michaux spent some time exploring and collecting in the American Midwest and in Canada, and it was not until the summer of 1794 that he returned to the southern Appalachians. This was to be his last visit to the Black Mountains. He again used Ainsworth's home in Turkey Cove as a base from which to make his excursions. After collecting on Linville Mountain, Michaux reached "sur le cote . . . de Black Mountain" (the . . . side of Black Mountain) on August 10. The blank space in the quoted passage appears in Michaux's handwritten journal, so it will never be known with certainty which portion of the Black Mountains he botanized. But from the trees he noted—red spruce, striped or Pennsylvania maple, and mountain ash—it can be concluded that he explored the northern deciduous and spruce-fir forests at an elevation of at least 4,000 or 5,000 feet.

As with his other trips to the Black Mountains, it is not known whether Michaux reached any summits during his 1794 visit. He was unaware that the Black Mountains formed the highest range in the eastern United States. Indeed, after leaving the Black Mountains Michaux climbed to the summit of Grandfather Mountain and proclaimed in his journal that that mountain was "the most elevated of all those [mountains] which form the chain of the Alleghanies and the Appalachians." Such a belief was, no doubt, merely adopted from the local inhabitants. Four decades would elapse before a scientist—who was influenced indirectly by Michaux's journals—would correctly designate the Black Mountains as the highest mountain range in the eastern United States.

André Michaux left America in 1796. Upon reaching France, he began work on a monograph on American oaks and an even more scientifically important two-volume work on the flora of North America. These books and the numerous plants he discovered (many of which presently bear his name) are Michaux's legacy. In 1802, while on a botanical expedition to Madagascar, Michaux succumbed to a tropical fever.

In the tradition of the Bartrams, Michaux's son, Francois André (1770-1855), took up the profession of his father. Like the elder Michaux, Francois André made significant contributions to the science of botany in the United States. His major work, a three-volume series entitled *The Forest Trees of North America*, earned him the title of "Father of American Forestry." More important to the history of the Black Mountains, however, was the younger Michaux's narrative description of his *Travels to the West of the Alleghany Mountains*, a volume published in 1805. In that work he stated:

It is here [in North Carolina] that the Alleghanies, which cross the United States for the space of nine hundred miles, have the highest elevation. This is the opinion of most of the inhabitants, who, from the mountainous part of Pennsylvania and Virginia, have emigrated on the confines of North Carolina, and who know the respective heights of all these mountains. That of the first rank is called Grandfather Mountain, the next Iron Mountain [a range that contains Roan Mountain], and thus in succession Yellow Mountain, Black Mountain, and Table Mountain, which are all situated upon the western rivers.

Although the younger Michaux had no way of knowing that the rankings he gave were inaccurate, he was aware that the elevations of North Carolina mountains had not yet been ascertained. Ironically, while F. A. Michaux apparently never visited the Black Mountains, it was he, not his father, who was to influence more directly the subsequent history of the range.

Many other botanists and plant collectors were active in the southern Appalachians from the late 1700s to the mid-1800s. From England, John Fraser and his son explored the region during the same

Francois André Michaux (1770-1855) was the son of the renowned French botanist André Michaux, the first man known to have explored the Black Mountains. Through his writings the younger Michaux was to influence future exploration of the range. Portrait of Michaux by Rembrandt Peale; reproduced in Henry Savage, Jr., *Lost Heritage* (New York: William Morrow and Company, 1970), p. 224.

time period in which their French counterparts and rivals, the Michauxs, were present there. It was for John Fraser that the Fraser's fir, the most abundant tree along the crest of the Black Mountains (and other high ranges), was named. Their collection and introduction into England of this tree and other plants from elevated habitats suggest that the Frasers did reach the upper elevations of southern Appalachian peaks; however, the written record is too sketchy to demonstrate whether or not they actually botanized in the Black Mountains. Of the numerous botanists active in the southern Appalachians, only a few are actually known to have collected in the Black Mountains—Moses Ashley Curtis in 1839 and 1854, Samuel Botsford Buckley[2] in 1842, and Lewis Reeve Gibbes[3] in the 1850s. (Mt. Gibbes, at the southern end of the Black Mountains, was named for L. R. Gibbes.) But by the time Buckley and Gibbes made their excursions, the grand period of botanical exploration in the southern Appalachians was coming to a close.

III

Elisha Mitchell and His Early Trips
to the Black Mountains

Science has always played an important part in the history of the Black Mountains, as it has for many mountain ranges. Both directly and indirectly, scientific exploration was responsible for making the range known to the outside world. While botany was the first science to be investigated in the Black Mountains, it was physical geography— particularly the measuring of mountain elevations—that was to have the greatest impact on the history of the range.

Although others would develop the science more extensively, it was Elisha Mitchell, a professor at the University of North Carolina, who pioneered the knowledge of physical geography in the Black Mountains. Unlike the Michauxs, Elisha Mitchell was a native of America, born in the hills of northwest Connecticut on August 19, 1793. He came from a family of substantial means, which afforded him the opportunity to attend Yale College. Mitchell distinguished himself at Yale, and upon graduating in 1813 he took charge of a nearby girls' school, where he met his future wife, Maria S. North. In 1816 he returned to Yale, where he earned a master of arts degree. After receiving an honorary doctor of divinity degree in 1840, he was usually referred to as "Dr. Mitchell."

Almost all of Elisha Mitchell's adult years were spent in North Carolina as a professor of the sciences at the state university in Chapel Hill. When he first arrived in 1818, the University of North Carolina consisted only of a president, 3 professors, and 92 students, in contrast to the institution's present enrollment of more than 20,000 students. His initial appointment in 1818 was in mathematics and natural philosophy, which included the teaching of botany, zoology, and some physical sciences. In 1825 he gave up that position to take on the university's only other science professorship—in chemistry,

Elisha Mitchell (1793-1857), an educator, minister, and scientist, was the first individual to concern himself with determining the elevations of some of North Carolina's high mountains. Portrait of Mitchell by Nathaniel Jocelyn, signed and dated 1851; reproduced from Laura MacMillan (comp.), *The North Carolina Portrait Index, 1700-1860* (Chapel Hill: University of North Carolina Press, 1963), p. 164.

geology, and mineralogy—which he held until his death in 1857. Mitchell's zeal for work also resulted in his taking on the duties of burser for the university, superintendent of its buildings and grounds, and lecturer in a number of nonscientific subjects including Latin, logic, history, geography, and composition. In addition, he was ordained as a Presbyterian minister in 1821; and he preached regularly both at the university and at a local church. For one year—1835—he served as acting president of the university following the death of the previous president, Joseph Caldwell, in January of that year.

Like many scientists of his day, Elisha Mitchell was a generalist. He was noted for his extensive knowledge in a number of fields. He was without question one of the best-read men in the state. His personal library contained 1,900 books, the greatest number dealing with chemistry, geology, mineralogy, botany, horticulture, geography and travel, history, and theology. He subscribed to more than a dozen scientific journals, including the *American Journal of Science and Arts* (Silliman's Journal). In this periodical, Mitchell published articles on a wide variety of subjects, including "Storms and Meteorological Observations," "The Geology of the Gold Region of North Carolina," and "The Effect of Matter in Modifying the Force of Chemical Attraction." For his students, he published three textbooks that ranged in size from a 27-page work on natural history to a several-hundred-page volume on chemistry. A conservative scientist, Mitchell was not inclined to initiate new scientific theories or discoveries. Because of this and his desire to be knowledgeable in many fields, he never attained a worldwide reputation in any particular science. His renown within the state, however, was such that in 1883 a North Carolina-based scientific society, appropriately concerned with all the sciences, was named for him.

As a scientist, Mitchell was interested in all three geographic regions of his adopted state; but it was his work in the mountain region, particularly in the Black Mountains, for which he is most famous. An interest in the North Carolina mountains probably developed soon after his arrival in Chapel Hill, but it was quite a few years before he actually made his first trip into the region. In 1825 he took charge of the North Carolina Geological Survey, the first statewide survey to be organized anywhere in the nation. It was while fulfilling the duties of this survey, during the summers of 1827 and 1828, that he made his first two trips west of the Blue Ridge.

Mitchell's 1827 and 1828 trips were to inspire him to return to the area in 1835 for the purpose of measuring some of its mountain elevations. In 1827 he had obtained his first glimpse of the Black Mountains from the vicinity of Morganton; and even then he noted that the range appeared to be higher than Grandfather Mountain, which at that time was assumed to be the highest point in the mountain region. The following year, accompanied by a friend and two local inhabitants, he ascended Grandfather Mountain. From its summit, he compared the elevations of the mountains in view:

It was a question with us [he wrote] whether the Black and Roan Mountains were not higher than the Grandfather and we were all inclined to give them the palm. . . . There can be no doubt that the country around the base of the Grandfather is higher than any other tract along these elevations but I suspect the Black and Roan to be higher peaks.

In a brief parenthetical comment made in an 1829 geological report, Mitchell stated that he felt the Black Mountains probably contained the highest land between the Gulf of Mexico and the White Mountains of New Hampshire, a range widely regarded as including the highest peaks in the East.

In 1835 Mitchell returned to the mountains of western North Carolina to make a more accurate determination of their true elevations. This became the first of five trips the professor was to make to the Black Mountain range. Not only did Mitchell's own 1827 and 1828 travels in western North Carolina prompt such a trip, but several individuals also were instrumental. One of these was Francois André Michaux, whose *Travels to the West of the Alleghany Mountains* Mitchell had read—probably prior to making his sojourns of 1827 and 1828. Another influence on Mitchell was David Lowry Swain

David Lowry Swain (1801-1868), North Carolina governor and later president of the state university in Chapel Hill, encouraged Elisha Mitchell to ascertain the elevations of North Carolina mountains. Engraving of Swain from John Preston Arthur, *Western North Carolina: A History* (Raleigh: Edwards and Broughton Printing Company, 1914), facing p. 420.

(1801-1868), a governor of North Carolina during the early 1830s and later president of the state university. Swain, a native of Buncombe County, wanted to encourage any activity that would bring recognition to western North Carolina; and measuring the height of its mountains certainly seemed to qualify.

Although the determination of mountain elevations was important to Mitchell during his 1835 journey, he also hoped to trace geological boundaries and determine the positions of prominent landscape features through a trigonometric survey.[4] In a memorandum book, he noted the wide variety of subjects he hoped to study:

Objects of attention—Geology; Botany; Height of the Mountains; Positions by Trigonometry; Woods, as of the Fir, Spruce, Magnolia, Birch; Fish, especially Trout; Springs; Biography, &c. . . . [Objects taken included] Two Barometers, a Quadrant, a Vasculum for plants, and a Hammer for rocks.

With these ambitious goals in mind, Mitchell left his Chapel Hill home in late June and headed for the mountains of western North Carolina. Probably traveling by means of a one-horse wagon, he reached Morganton in about a week. There he established a base station and, by making barometric observations over several days, concluded the town's elevation to be 968 feet above sea level. Mitchell could then use his base elevation to ascertain the elevations of various mountaintops by having an acquaintance take barometric readings in Morganton at approximately the same time that he was taking readings on mountain summits. By means of a complex mathematical formula, the difference between each of those readings could be used to arrive at estimated heights for the respective mountaintops. Measuring elevations by barometer was advantageous in that a number of readings could be made in the course of a few weeks, but the method had its drawbacks with regard to accuracy, especially if only a single reading was taken at each location.

Leaving his base in Morganton, Mitchell took to horseback to begin his examination of various western North Carolina mountains. He first visited the Linville Gorge area, where he passed by Table Rock and descended to Linville Falls. He next ascended Grandfather Mountain and Roan Mountain, taking elevation measurements on both peaks. The relative ease with which Roan Mountain could be ascended was especially appreciated by the professor after the difficult ascent he had experienced on Grandfather Mountain.

Mitchell then headed southward to the Black Mountains, where he spent the greatest portion of his time—almost a week. He first established himself at the home of Thomas Young, a farmer who lived along the South Toe River near present-day Micaville. From there, Young and a hired guide named Green Silver accompanied Mitchell to the summit of what is presently known as Celo Knob, at the north-

24

Celo Knob (*upper left*), the northeastern end of the Black Mountains, was the first peak in the range to be ascended by Elisha Mitchell. The town of Burnsville, visible in the foreground of this modern-day view, had been established as the county seat of Yancey County only one year prior to Mitchell's 1835 visit. Photograph (1978) by the author.

eastern end of the Black Mountains. The elevation Mitchell calculated for Celo Knob, 5,946 feet, was somewhat lower than the elevation he had determined for Roan Mountain—just the reverse of what is presently known about their relative elevations. Celo Knob was considered by some local inhabitants to be the highest in the vicinity, but once on its summit Mitchell noted that there were Black Mountain "peaks considerably more elevated farther South."

Mitchell did not then try to traverse those peaks but instead descended Celo Knob and made his way up the Cane River valley to a location closer to the heart of the Black Mountain range. He stopped at the farm of Samuel Austin near the confluence of Cattail Creek and Cane River. Accompanied by Austin and one of Austin's neighbors, William Wilson, Mitchell ascended Yeates Knob, a peak his guides apparently believed to have been the highest in that vicinity.

Once atop Yeates Knob, Mitchell once again realized, either by sight alone or by means of a simple water level,[5] that he had not reached the highest point of the Black Mountains. Even though clear weather and a good location afforded him an excellent view of the full length of the Black Mountain range, it was difficult for him to determine which peak was the highest. He explained the problem in these words:

25

The western arm of the Black Mountains, as viewed from N.C. Highway 128 south of Mt. Mitchell, reaches its highest elevation at Yeates Knob. This point was the object of Elisha Mitchell's second ascent of the Black Mountains in 1835. Photograph (1978) by the author.

It is a matter of considerable difficulty, in the case of a long ridge like this, that swells here and there into a knob two or three hundred feet higher than its neighbors, to ascertain which it is that overtops the rest, from our inability to determine how much of the apparent elevation of one, amongst a number, is due to its nearness, & how much to height.

In an informal note made public twenty years after the ascent, Mitchell described his view of the eastern or main arm of the Black Mountain range as seen from Yeates Knob:

Counting [southward] from Young's knob [Celo Knob]: one low one; one low one; two in one, the northernmost pointed; a round knob, same height; a double knob; then the highest; then a long, low place, with a knob in it; then a round three knobby knob, equal to the highest; after which the ridge descends.

In this excerpt, Mitchell identified two "highest" points: present-day Mt. Mitchell and the Mt. Gibbes-Clingman's Peak-Potato Knob complex. In a statement published soon after his 1835 trip, he indicated which of these two points he actually believed to be the highest:

Two were very nearly equal, but the one at the head of the ridge between the North and Middle forks of Caney River, was finally fixed upon as the highest.

Inasmuch as the tributaries that form below the Mt. Gibbes-Clingman's Peak-Potato Knob complex could not possibly represent

26

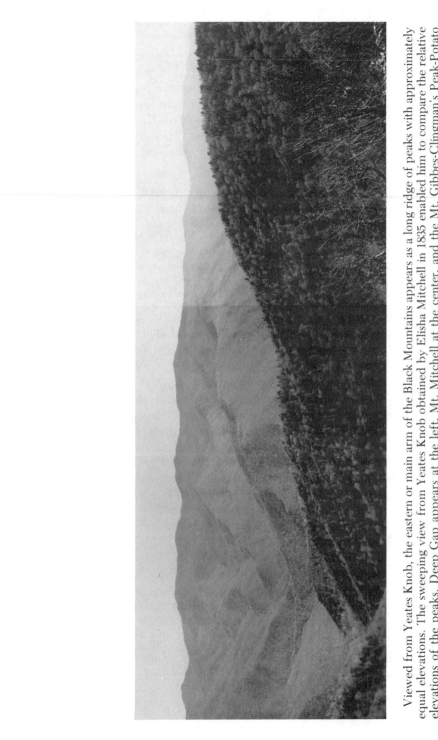

Viewed from Yeates Knob, the eastern or main arm of the Black Mountains appears as a long ridge of peaks with approximately equal elevations. The sweeping view from Yeates Knob obtained by Elisha Mitchell in 1835 enabled him to compare the relative elevations of the peaks. Deep Gap appears at the left, Mt. Mitchell at the center, and the Mt. Gibbes-Clingman's Peak-Potato Knob Complex at the right. Composite view from photographs (1975) made by the author.

the "North" or "Middle" forks of Cane River, Mitchell must have been indicating that present-day Mt. Mitchell was the highest peak in the Black Mountains.

After taking an elevation measurement for Yeates Knob, Mitchell descended to the Cane River valley. The following morning, July 28, he set out for the peak he had identified as the highest from Yeates Knob. He was accompanied by William Wilson and Adoniram Allen, who, like Wilson, had taken up settlement on the lower portion of Cattail Creek near its confluence with the Cane River. As described by Wilson more than twenty years later, the route of their historic ascent was as follows:

We went from my house up to the Green Ponds,[6] then we crossed the left hand, or Sugar Camp Fork, and kept up the right hand side of the creek pretty well up to opposite the Beech Nursery. We then turned to the left across the same fork, (Sugar Camp,) and took up the Little Piney Mountain, and kept directly up that ridge to the top of the Black. We came to the top at a small glade, not more than a quarter of an acre in extent, and turning to the right, not more than one hundred and fifty yards, we arrived on top of the main highest peak, being the same one as we thought that we had selected from Yeates's Knob the day before. . . . In going up the mountain, I remember that we stopped at the last place where we crossed the creek to get water, and the Doctor forgot his notebook in which he set down his figures, and during our ascent, he would, from time to time, set his barometer and call upon myself and Adoniram Allen . . . to assist him in remembering the numbers. . . . We had great difficulty in getting up, as the way was exceedingly rough.

As was true of Elisha Mitchell's two previous ascents of the Black Mountains, this one was made on foot. The steep terrain and dense undergrowth would not permit an ascent by horseback, and the only trails that existed were animal trails. In an article written for the *Raleigh Register* in November, 1835, Mitchell described the difficulty of his ascent, focusing particularly on a bear trail he was obliged to follow, probably on his hands and knees in some places:

The roughness of the sides and top of the Black Mountain is likely to prevent his being often ascended from motives of curiosity and pleasure. A route, very much better than that pursued by us, is not likely to be discovered, and *that* can be accomplished only on foot; and for between one and two miles, it is thro' thick laurels and along a bear trail. . . . The Bear, in passing up and down the Mountain, finds it wisest to keep the ridges, and trampling down the young laurels as they spring up, breaking the limbs from the old ones and pushing them aside, he forms at last a sort of burrow above ground, through this bed of vegetation, along which he passes without difficulty. This is a bear trail; which though an excellent kind of turnpike probably in view of the animal that formed it, is much less highly approved by the two-legged animal who tries it after him, and who submits with some degree of shame and indignation to the fashion of the place in regard to the attitude he assumes as he travels up and down the mountain.

28

In contrast to his earlier ascents of the Black Mountains, Mitchell found the summit of present-day Mt. Mitchell enveloped in fog, limiting visibility to only a couple of hundred yards. He thus was unable to determine either his location or relative elevation with regard to nearby peaks. Poor visibility did not, however, prevent him from taking the barometric pressure (23.807 inches) and the temperature (58 degrees F.) atop Mt. Mitchell. By comparing these data with the corresponding data for Morganton (28.95 inches and 81 degrees F.) at approximately the same time, Mitchell later determined the elevation of what he called "the Highest Peak of the Black" to be 5,508 feet above Morganton or 6,476 feet above sea level.

After spending about two hours on Mt. Mitchell's summit, the professor began his descent. He and Allen pursued approximately the same course they had taken in going up, while Wilson took another route. The round-trip distance of the route Mitchell followed from Cattail Creek to Mt. Mitchell was about eighteen miles; and with a difference in elevation of about 3,800 feet between the two points, it is no wonder that the professor admitted to being "thoroughly fatigued" at day's end.

The summer vacation period at the University of North Carolina lasted only six weeks, and Mitchell's time was running short. After a brief return to Roan Mountain to recalculate its elevation, he began the week-long journey to Chapel Hill.

Although Mitchell had ambitious goals for tracing the geological boundaries of the mountain region and obtaining accurate geographic positions by means of a trigonometric survey, it appears that during his 1835 trip he devoted the bulk of his scientific attention to measuring the elevations of mountains. In so doing he made his greatest accomplishment: he demonstrated scientifically that the Black Mountains contained the highest peak measured in the United States up to that time. Mitchell's announcement of the range's superlative height was first made public in a lengthy article that appeared in the *Raleigh Register* on November 3, 1835:

The Black Mountain [range] . . . has some Peaks of greater elevation than any point that has hitherto been measured in North-America, East of the Rocky Mountains, and is believed to be the highest Mountain in the United States.[7]

While Mitchell realized that his discovery was of some significance, he does not seem to have anticipated the attention it received both at home and at distant locations. The editor of the *Raleigh Register* made the following observation:

Had we learned from a less respectable source, that the highest Mountain in the United States was to be found in North Carolina, we could not have believed the fact! . . . The fact itself is not so astonishing, as that the discovery of it should not have been sooner made.

After notices of Mitchell's discovery appeared in such notable newspapers as the *Charleston Mercury*, the *Baltimore Chronicle*, and the *Boston Recorder*, the editor of the *Register* declared:

Humble as are the pretensions of our State, it is nevertheless a source of much gratification, that we have it now in our power, to LOOK DOWN upon such of our arrogant sisters of the Confederacy[8] as may insolently venture to taunt us with inferiority.

In spite of the notices that appeared in newspapers throughout the United States, many gazetteers, geographies, and maps continued to show New Hampshire's Mt. Washington as the highest peak in eastern America. Even after a condensed version of Mitchell's 1835 article appeared in the *American Journal of Science and Arts* in 1839, there seems to have been very little dissemination of the claim that North Carolina's Black Mountains were superior in height. Geographers gradually came to recognize the greater height of the Black Mountains; however, even at the present time many individuals living outside the Southeast still erroneously believe Mt. Washington to be the highest point in the East.

The actual elevation of Mt. Mitchell, as the highest peak in the Black Mountains came to be called, is now known to be 6,684 feet above sea level—208 feet higher than Elisha Mitchell determined it to be. Had Mitchell correctly ascertained Morganton's elevation—it is actually 1,182 feet above sea level instead of 968, as the professor believed—his calculation for the high peak would have been 6,690 feet, just 6 feet more than its actual elevation. The relative accuracy of Mitchell's calculation was merely coincidental, however, since the half-dozen other points that he measured during his 1835 trip differed by up to 500 feet from their presently recognized elevations.

Mitchell returned to the mountains of western North Carolina again during the summer of 1838. In contrast to his 1835 excursion, his two 1838 ascents of the Black Mountains originated in the valleys of Buncombe County instead of Yancey County. Establishing his base in Asheville, he first approached the Black Mountains by way of Dillingham's Cove in the vicinity of present-day Barnardsville. Accompanied by a guide, he ascended Bullhead Mountain, located in the Great Craggy range about three miles south of its junction with the Black Mountain range. He followed the ridgeline of the Great Craggies and probably the Black Mountains to a point "not far from Yeate's Knob" and stated that he "saw the high peak [of the Black Mountains] distinctly once more." Oddly, he later professed that at that time he became "fully satisfied that I was not upon the highest point in the Black Mountain ridge in 1835." The professor gave no indication as to how he came to believe this.

Upon returning to Dillingham's Cove, Mitchell decided to approach the range from the valley of the North Fork of the Swannanoa River. Enlisting Frederic Burnett for a guide, he ascended by foot the southern end of the Black Mountains to the mountain complex that consists of the points presently called Potato Knob, Clingman's Peak, and Mt. Gibbes. On one of the latter two peaks, which are almost equal in elevation, he barometrically determined an altitude of 6,581 feet above sea level. This figure differs by only about 30 feet from the actual elevations of these two peaks, which makes it the most accurate of any of Elisha Mitchell's elevation measurements in the Black Mountains.

In 1844 Mitchell made his third trip to the range. Certainly, one reason for this visit was the doubt that had entered his mind as to whether he had ever ascended the highest summit in 1835. Concerning this trip, he stated:

> I determined to try the Black once more, in which mountain I was well satisfied that the highest points are to be found, as I was, also, that I had never yet been upon the highest.

Both in the Black Mountains and at other locations in western North Carolina, Mitchell desired to put to use a new type of mountain barometer that he had acquired from Paris. In addition, the professor hoped to make observations on the state's expanding mining activity.

Leaving Chapel Hill in mid-June, Mitchell investigated gold, lead, and silver mines in the piedmont. Once in the mountains, he spent some time visiting mines and determining elevations in the region west of Asheville. In contrast to his previous mountain visits, he limited his measuring to lower-elevation locations along the roads he traveled. After a week to ten days of such investigations, the professor began preparations for the final leg of his 1844 trip—a visit to the Black Mountains.

Mitchell established his barometric base in Asheville, where he asked his friend Dr. John Dickson to monitor a barometer while he, Mitchell, was in the Black Mountains. On July 5 Mitchell left Asheville en route to the range by way of Burnsville and the Cane River valley. The day following his arrival in Burnsville was a Sunday, and he took advantage of the opportunity to preach a sermon prior to his ascent. In a letter written that day, he told his wife that he was not exactly looking forward to the trip planned for the following day. He wrote:

> To morrow I am expecting to ascend the Black Mountain I hope for the last time. I shall probably now reach the highest summit.

In the Cane River valley, Mitchell obtained the services of William Riddle and Riddle's son to accompany and guide him on his ascent.

(Contrary to what has been commonly stated, "Big Tom" Wilson did not serve as a guide for Mitchell during this ascent.) On July 8 Mitchell and the two Riddles began what the fifty-year-old professor called "the hardest day's work I ever performed." In a letter written to his wife on July 14, he provided his personal description of the ascent:

That dreadful journey to the top of the mountain. Caney [Cane] River drains a basin partly encircled by the mountain [range]. I went up the main stream—then up a fork and over the spruce pine mountain ridge to another fork—then over another high mountain ridge to a third for[k] by which time it was between 12 and 1. and all the way through laurels, and I had still the whole Black mountain before me. I could not help thinking as I crawled along over the leaves under a shelving rock what a comfortable place it would be to die in. Reached the top at 4.

Mitchell's comment about a place in which to die proved prophetic.

In an article published twelve years later, William Riddle gave the following description of their 1844 route of ascent:

[We] went from [my] house on Caney River, by way of the Green ponds, and there took up a ridge to a place called the beach [sic] nursery, and from thence turned to the right and went in a southerly direction as direct a course as possible to that part of the [Black] Mountain since called Mount Gibbes, near Mount Mitchell [present-day Clingman's Peak].

Contrary to Mitchell's belief, the peak he ascended in 1844 was not the highest in the range but was instead Mt. Gibbes, three miles to the south of the high peak. Both his own 1844 description and the one given by Riddle in 1856 (after a few more place names had come into existence) indicate that the peak they ascended in 1844 was one at the southern end of the range in the Mt. Gibbes-Clingman's Peak-Potato Knob complex. The ridge mentioned by Mitchell ("the spruce pine mountain ridge") rose above the Green Ponds. Crossing this ridge from the north to the south and passing over two additional streams with a ridge between them, Mitchell could only have been heading to a peak at the southern end of the range. Had the professor wanted to reach what was actually the highest peak in the range—Mt. Mitchell—he would have followed, not crossed, "the spruce pine mountain ridge" to its upper end, where it joined the main Black Mountain ridgeline, and then he would have taken that ridgeline to the high peak one-half mile northeast.

Mitchell spent only a short time on the summit of Mt. Gibbes, just long enough to take a reading with his new mountain barometer. From that reading, he later calculated the elevation of the peak to be 6,672 feet above sea level—about 125 feet higher than the actual elevation.

Mitchell and the two Riddles tried to descend as much of the mountain as they could before darkness overtook them. In a letter written to his wife, the professor gave the following personal account of the descent:

Descended to the river by about sundown—Jumped along the rocks down the bed of the river, got some dreadful falls and soused in till it was dark—a heavy rain which further aided in wetting me through and through—then turned up into the woods— made three unsuccessful trials before we could get fire—finally fired a poplar stump and slept by the side of it on the wet ground and some wet moss we collected in my wet clothes—and seem now to be none the worse for it.

According to William Riddle, they traveled only as far as a point opposite the Beech Nursery (presently known as Beech Nursery Gap) before darkness set in. The next morning they followed what Riddle considered to be the main stream of the Cane River (Beech Nursery Creek). They eventually reached Riddle's home, ending an exhausting round trip of about twenty miles. Mitchell then set out on a direct course for Chapel Hill.

Mitchell's only publication resulting from his 1844 trip appeared the following year in the Asheville *Highland Messenger* and in the *Raleigh Register*. In the article, the professor provided the first accurate delineation of the Black Mountain range with regard to its length, shape, and boundaries:

The Black Mountain . . . is a long curved ridge, 15 or 20 miles in length, its base having somewhat the form of a common fishhook, of which the extremity of the shank is near Thomas Young's, in Yancey. It sweeps round by the heads of the South fork of Toe, the Swannanoe [sic], Reem's Creek and Ivy, and ends at the Big Butt, or Yeatis' [sic] Knob—Caney River drains by a number of forks the hollow of the curve.

Curiously, Mitchell gave only passing mention to the 6,672-foot measurement he had taken in the range, noting only that it had been obtained at the "Top of Black." In his article he dealt primarily with the subject of husbandry, the development of which he urged not only for the valleys of Yancey County but also for its mountain heights:

The tops of the mountains also, where the ridge is broad or a single summit has a rounded surface instead of a sharp peak, will afford a few grazing farms. I do not altogether despair of living to see the time when the highest summit of the Black shall be enclosed and covered with a fine coat of the richest grasses, and when the cheese of Yancey shall rival in the market of the lower counties that which is imported from other States.

While Elisha Mitchell was appreciative of natural beauty, he was also one to search constantly for practical uses for land. In Mitchell's view, land could be both beautiful and productive. Partially fulfilling the professor's hope, portions of the Black Mountains were soon to be used for open (unfenced) grazing land—a use that continued for more than half a century. Along with this indicator of expanding settlement around the Black Mountains, developments of a different sort were also to penetrate the wilderness of the highest mountains in the eastern United States.

IV

The 1850s: A Decade of Developing Tourism

The relative isolation of western North Carolina during the 1830s and 1840s limited travel to the Black Mountains and to the region as a whole. With a few exceptions, traveling conditions throughout North Carolina's mountain region were primitive, and most roads (or tracks, as they would be regarded at the present time) were used for little more than the necessities of trade. Outside the immediate area, only a small segment of the population had any substantial familiarity with the mountain region. Of those who had heard of western North Carolina's assets, some gradually made their way into the region to find out firsthand what it had to offer.

Most visitors who went to western North Carolina did so to escape the oppressive summer heat and the infectious diseases of the southern lowlands. Many, no doubt, availed themselves of the relative luxury of two hot-springs resorts—Warm Springs in Madison County and Sulphur Springs in Buncombe County—which were developed during the 1830s. Relatively few excursionists, it appears, had a desire to ascend any of the region's high mountains. For those who did, the summits of Roan and Bald mountains were easily attainable by horseback. But, as Elisha Mitchell noted, individuals who desired to reach the height of the Black Mountains did not have it so easy. When a local inhabitant was asked how to reach the summit of the range, he wryly replied: "O! It's a very easy matter, stranger; you only have to *walk* about six miles, and right straight *up* the roughest country you ever *did* see."

Nevertheless, a few hardy excursionists did make ascents of the Black Mountains during the 1830s and 1840s. As previously noted, one such ascent was made by botanist Moses Ashley Curtis in 1839. Like Elisha Mitchell, Curtis found the task a difficult one. He ascended the range from the South Toe valley, following a route different from any taken by Mitchell. Although the climb to the ridgeline seemed familiar to his two guides, their route down the mountain slopes was "unknown & untried." Curtis and his guides spent the first night of their excursion near the height of the ridgeline and the next day followed the ridge across what are believed to be Cattail Peak, Balsam Cone, Mt. Craig, and Mt. Mitchell. Soon after descending the range, Curtis wrote the following lines to his wife:

Thus was accomplished a feat which for hardship toil & real fatigue far surpassed any labor of [my] life. . . . The tremendous height of the [Black] Mt. cannot be realized til it is ascended. There the whole world seems spread below . . . & even old Grandfather & Roan are looked down upon as small things. No mountain[s] previously ascended [by] me are worth naming in the comparison, either for ruggedness or height.

As there were yet no trails in existence, visitors to the Black Mountains during the 1830s and 1840s began their ascents at a number of different locations. It seems likely that most of those who ascended the range during this period climbed from the North Fork valley to the peaks at the southern end of the range. In support of this belief, an observer noted in 1845 that some trees on the summit of Clingman's Peak had been cut, allowing a view, and that other trees had their bark carved with initials.

Land speculation in the Black Mountains presented what was perhaps the first foretaste of the range's ensuing development. In the early 1840s David L. Swain and Nicholas W. Woodfin, a prominent Buncombe County lawyer, purchased approximately 13,000 acres of land in the upper Cane River basin; the tract extended to the height of the Black Mountains. Swain's involvement was not for speculation but because he wanted to become an owner of the highest land in the eastern United States. The land never brought any great profit to Swain or Woodfin, but their acquisition of it did result in an 1845 survey that provided the most detailed and accurate description and map of the Black Mountains made up to that time. The survey was headed by Nehemiah Blackstock (b. 1795), a Buncombe County farmer and surveyor for whom Blackstock Knob (at the southern end of the Black Mountains) is named. Blackstock used his compass's level to determine correctly which peak was the highest in the range. Because his written description or map was never circulated publicly, however, the potential value of the survey was never realized.

The isolation and limited amount of travel in the Black Mountains during the 1830s and 1840s provided little indication of the dramatic change to come to the range during the 1850s. Because of the general prosperity that existed throughout North Carolina, substantial improvements in transportation and communication were possible. By word of mouth and by articles published in newspapers, magazines, and books, more and more people were becoming aware of the attractions offered by North Carolina's mountain region. Improved roads enabled people to reach western North Carolina more quickly and easily. By the end of the decade, stagecoaches were going to Asheville from all directions, and the Western North Carolina Railroad had been laid to within fifty miles of the Blue Ridge.

Many early visitors to western North Carolina came from Charleston; consequently, it is not surprising that it was a Charlestonian, William Patton, who inaugurated development in the Black Mountains. Patton (1794-1858) was a native of Wilkes County, North Carolina, but he had spent most of his adult life in Charleston, where he became a prosperous merchant and land speculator. Patton had strong ties to North Carolina's mountains—not only because of his appreciation of the region's scenery and climate but also because his uncle and cousin lived in the area. Interestingly, these men were the primary developers and operators of the Warm Springs health resort and Asheville's Eagle Hotel during the early to mid-1800s. Thus, even before William Patton made his presence known in western North Carolina, the Patton family had made a considerable impact on the development of tourism in the region.

Sometime around 1840 Patton became a summer resident of the Asheville area and began to take an interest in the Black Mountains.

In the early 1850s William Patton (1794-1858), a prosperous merchant from Charleston, South Carolina, made the first significant improvements to facilitate tourist travel to the Black Mountains. Portrait and silhouette of Patton in the possession (1978) of Miss Edith Holmes, Asheville, a descendant of Patton; photographs supplied by the author.

In 1845 he purchased 740 acres of land at the upper end of the North Fork valley, and in 1850 he acquired a 4,000-acre tract on the southern slope of the range up to the ridgeline at Potato and Blackstock knobs. While Patton saw his Black Mountain land as a good investment, his major concern seems to have been the establishment of a second home amid the beauty of the mountains.

On his lower tract, above the upper limit of North Fork settlement, Patton built two cabins. They were spaced about a mile apart, and each was located at a spring near the waters of the Right Fork of the North Fork. The upper cabin, which became known as the "Depot," was constructed in 1850 at an elevation of approximately 3,200 feet. In order to reach his cabins by buggy, Patton extended the primitive road that had been cut to the upper portion of the North Fork valley.

Unlike the North Fork settlers, Patton saw no reason why development should be limited to the valley. He thus proceeded to build a third cabin at an elevation of 5,200 feet, where he could find cooler temperatures and more distant views. Located along a spur ridge off Potato Knob, this highest cabin of William Patton became known as the "Mountain House." The building, erected in 1851 by J. M. Owens and W. Keenan of Asheville, consisted of two stories and a basement. It was a rustic structure, measuring 20 by 50 feet, with a portico facing southeast. The foundation and chimneys were constructed of rock, while the main body of the house was formed with hand-hewn and notched balsam logs. Both the wood and rock were readily available at that elevation. Each story was divided by a hall, with rooms and fireplaces on each side. Interior furnishings appear to have been simple.

To reach the Mountain House from his lower cabins, Patton had a two-mile-long horse trail constructed. Because of the trail's steepness, numerous switchbacks were necessary, prompting one early traveler to remark that it was "as crooked and seven times more so than the ram-horn that blew down the walls of Jericho." The horse trail extended one to two miles past the Mountain House to the peaks at the southern end of the Black Mountains. Thus, in 1851, for the first time in the history of the range, some of the highest points in the Black Mountains could be reached with relative ease and comfort.

At the same time William Patton was making his improvements on the southern slopes of the Black Mountains, accommodations for excursionists were being developed within the North Fork valley. Among the valleys that surround the Black Mountains, the North Fork was perhaps best suited for the comfort and convenience of tourists. The valley was close to a major east-west route into the mountain region, and its population and level of development seem to have been more extensive than that of any of the other valleys surrounding the range. About 1850 Jesse Stepp, a North Fork farmer,

It was through the North Fork (of the Swannanoa) valley that the greatest number of excursionists traveled to the Black Mountains during the mid- and late nineteenth century. At the present time, a portion of the valley is filled by the Burnett Reservoir, the main water supply for the city of Asheville. Photograph (1976) by the author.

erected several cabins to accommodate the increasing number of visitors. Throughout the decade, Stepp's lodgings, located at the upper end of the North Fork valley at the confluence of the Right Fork and the North Fork, served as a beginning point for excursions into the Black Mountains. At Stepp's, visitors could acquire guides and saddle horses for the trip to the peaks at the southern end of the range.

Patton's Mountain House may originally have been built for his own personal use and that of his friends, but by 1854 Patton decided to open it to the general public as a lodging establishment. It appears that he was motivated more by a desire to bring greater public attention to the Black Mountain range than by an interest in making profits. The Mountain House was generally open each year during the summer and early fall, the period during which it would receive the greatest use. The small size of the house limited the number of guests it could serve at any one time, but over the course of a season it could and did accommodate several hundred people. Beginning in 1854, Patton leased the Mountain House to a Mrs. Sarah Garenflo, who managed it for several years. During her tenure, at least, a guest could partake of champagne from France or salmon from Scotland, belying the lodge's rustic appearance and isolated location.

The following advertisement for the Mountain House, published in the *Asheville News* in 1854, provides insight into why people were attracted to the Black Mountains and how one could go about reaching their high peaks:

39

The Mountain House became an important stopover for excursionists who ascended the Black Mountains in the 1850s. The lodge, shown here, consisted of two stories and a basement, with fireplaces and a southeast-facing portico. This illustration, made after the demise of the structure, is not particularly accurate. Engraving from Edward King, *The Southern States of North America* (London: Blackie and Son, 1875), p. 511.

THERMOMETER RANGES FROM 56 TO 70, AND BLANKETS NECESSARY AT NIGHT IN THE HOTTEST OF SUMMER

Mrs. GARENFLO informs her friends and the public, that she has made arrangements with Mr. Wm. Patton, of Charleston—the owner of this property, to open the BLACK MOUNTAIN HOUSE, on Thursday, 13th July, 1854, and will do the best she can to make visiters [*sic*] and boarders comfortable. The house is on the top of the mountain, and 1½ to two miles from the highest peaks, which are 261 feet higher than Mount Washington—the highest of the White Mountains in New Hampshire—and consequently the highest mountain in the United States East of the Mississippi.

This mountain is 20 miles N.E. of Asheville, N.C. The road to it winds up the Swannanoa river—of which the Spring at the House is the head source. There are several good farm Houses for accommodation, on the Road and near the base of the mountain; and at the foot, particularly, Mr. Jesse Stapp [*sic*] has put up new buildings, and prepared to accommodate a large number of visiters. Mountain Trout fishing, bear, deer, and other hunting can be enjoyed here in season. Carriages can go safely as far as Mr. Stapp's at the foot of the mountain, where guides and saddle horses can be procured, for the 4 miles to the Mountain House and the 1½ to 2 miles to the main peaks. The [round-trip] excursion can be made in three days from Asheville. A regular hack will leave Asheville on Tuesday at 8 o'clock A.M., and returning leave Stapp's on Friday morning at 8 o'clock. Prices on the mountain, 50 cts each for supper and Breakfast; $1 for dinner, 35 to 37½ cts, for double or single beds; $2 per day or $10 a week for board; Horse feed 50¢ and all night $1. These rates are about double what is charged in the settlement. Those who ascend the mountain will learn the necessity for the increased charges.

Such advertisements no doubt attracted many summer residents and visitors as well as some permanent inhabitants of the area. Most visitors were probably from the southern states inasmuch as the North had its own mountains, and public awareness of opportunities to travel in the southern Appalachians was virtually nonexistent in the North. The advertisement's comparison of the height of the Black Mountains with that of the White Mountains of New Hampshire

From the early nineteenth century, Asheville could claim to be North Carolina's leading town west of the Blue Ridge. In 1850 the thriving community of 800 people accommodated travelers at several fine lodging establishments and served as the embarkation point for trips to the Black Mountains. Engraving, "View of Asheville, N.C. and the Mountains from the Summer House," 1851, courtesy North Carolina Collection, Pack Memorial Public Library; photograph supplied by the author.

41

In the 1850s hacks, or hired carriages, could be taken from Asheville via the North Fork valley to the base of the Black Mountains. Engraving from "A Winter in the South," Part 5, *Harper's New Monthly Magazine*, XVI (May, 1858), p. 721.

indicated not only that the superior height of the Black Mountains was a drawing card for visitors but also that knowledge of their superior height had still not become widely disseminated, even among southerners. In some ways, the development of the White Mountains paralleled that of the Black Mountains. Just two years before the Mountain House was opened to the public, a lodge of similar size was opened for visitors on the summit of Mt. Washington. Because that lodge was over 6,000 feet in elevation, Patton's Mountain House can perhaps best be characterized only as the highest full-service lodging establishment in the South.

The fact that the Black Mountains could be more easily reached than ever before was in part responsible for bringing a number of scientists and other prominent persons to the range during the 1850s. In addition to Elisha Mitchell, other scientists who visited the mountain range during the decade included Moses Ashley Curtis, Arnold Guyot, Joseph LeConte,[9] Ebenezer Emmons,[10] and Lewis R. Gibbes. United States Congressman Thomas L. Clingman and American historian George Bancroft also ascended the Black Mountains at this time.

It may seem curious that those who ascended the Black Mountains from the North Fork valley during the early 1850s were not being led to the highest peak in the range but only as far as the point presently known as Clingman's Peak, at the southern end of the range. The trail that had been built above the Mountain House in 1851 extended only to the height of the southernmost peaks of the Black Mountains. During the early 1850s a small log hut was built atop Clingman's Peak to shelter excursionists from the weather and to serve as an observation point.

In September, 1855, the belief that present-day Mt. Mitchell was the highest peak in the Black Mountains began to receive widespread attention. (This will be more fully described in Chapter V.) As a result, that very autumn, the trail from the North Fork valley to Clingman's Peak was extended three miles to the summit of Mt. Mitchell. From Clingman's Peak the new trail followed the Black Mountain ridge over Mt. Gibbes, down through Stepp's Gap, and over Mt. Hallback. A few hundred feet below the summit of Mt. Mitchell, visitors passed through a small glade of one or two acres. Since Jesse Stepp occupied this ridgetop land in September, 1855, he was probably the principal person involved in building the trail. About 1856, in the gap subsequently named for him, Stepp built a simple shelter and a spring-fed watering trough for those who rode on horseback to the high peak.

With the extension of the North Fork trail, the same sort of developments that had taken place earlier on Clingman's Peak began to occur on Mt. Mitchell. Either in late 1855 or 1856 the summit of the high peak was cleared of its timber and "a sort of rude observatory was constructed of pine [balsam] logs ten or twelve feet in height." Unlike Elisha Mitchell and the surveying party of Nehemiah Blackstock, persons visiting the mountaintop thereafter no longer were obliged to climb a balsam in order to obtain a view. As on Clingman's Peak, a shelter for visitors was built; however, it was separate from the observatory, being located about one hundred yards below the summit. Like the hut on Clingman's Peak, the shelter on Mt. Mitchell was primitively constructed, having only bark strips for the roof. It was built by Jesse Stepp at the same time the observatory was erected, apparently to provide overnight shelter to visitors who wished to view the sunset or sunrise from the high peak. A few food supplies and cooking and eating utensils were available in the cabin; but unlike the Mountain House, meals were a do-it-yourself affair between guides and visitors. The cabin was small, intended to accommodate comfortably no more than five or ten persons. It apparently sufficed quite adequately for most visitors to the mountain, but for a few the experience left a little to be desired. In the words of one member of a group of thirteen excursionists who stayed there in June, 1859:

We spent the night in a little hut near the top, and it was one of *the* nights. It rained nearly the whole time, the wind blew cold and made the most dreary, mournful sound among the old firs that I ever heard; the little cabin was so small that we could not even move after we had been packed in, and the fleas and other vermin were so thick you could almost stir them with a stick; the house leaked and smoked, and the wind whistled through the cracks as cold as December.

For sizable groups or those who declined to avail themselves of the cabin, a large overhanging cliff located nearby provided an adequate natural shelter.

In the late 1850s a crude cabin constructed on Mt. Mitchell's summit provided limited shelter for visitors. Engraving from "A Winter in the South," Part 3, p. 737.

Although the large majority of people who climbed the Black Mountains during the 1850s began their ascents in the North Fork valley, a few visits were begun in the Ivy, South Toe, or Cane river valleys. Of these valleys, the Cane River was the most frequently used. By the early 1850s the upper end of the valley had been settled to the point at which Sugarcamp Creek joins the river, and within a few years a road wide enough for a wagon extended southward from Burnsville to the vicinity of Cattail Creek. In contrast to the North Fork valley, no special accommodations were provided for the occasional visitor; but food and lodging were available at the cabins of local inhabitants. The price charged for room and board in at least one location in the Cane River valley was quite a bargain. In 1857 three men were quite pleased with the following goods and services they received from a resident of the valley:

Seventeen meals; one quart of honey; one peck of meal; cooking a ham and several pounds of bread; lodging for three; two gallons of milk and twenty pieces of washing. Charge—$2.25; and he said that he would knock off something if we were not entirely satisfied.

Sometime between late 1855 and mid-1857, a foot trail eight miles long was blazed to the summit of present-day Mt. Mitchell from the vicinity of the Green Ponds. This route led up the ridge of Big Spruce Pine Mountain (shown on the present United States Geological Survey topographic map as Big Pine Mountain and Wilson Ridge), through Beech Nursery Gap, and met the bridle trail from the North Fork of the Swannanoa at a point not far south of the summit of Mt. Mitchell.

Throughout the early and mid-1800s most visitors to the Black Mountains—scientists and excursionists alike—ascended the range with guides. According to Elisha Mitchell and Moses Ashley Curtis, the earliest of the guides were generally no more familiar with the territory than they were. For Mitchell and Curtis and for excursionists who came later, a major function of the guides was to carry supplies. By the 1850s local inhabitants had, no doubt, become more familiar with the range, but with the building of trails there was no longer any great need for guides to provide direction for visitors. Nevertheless, demand for guides continued, if not increased. Guides were hired for their knowledge of how to get along in the woods; for their familiarity with points of interest; and for their embodiment of the rural mountain character, which was alien to most excursionists. William Powers, one of the more prominent North Fork guides, was described as follows:

Bill has had quite a national reputation as a guide, having been to the high peak over one hundred times. He is a thorough mountaineer, understanding everything that should be done and the right way to do it—can do anything he ever saw done by another—knows everybody, their history,—all the news afloat and expresses himself in a style entirely peculiar to himself.

By the end of the 1850s, knowledge of the Black Mountains was becoming more widespread, with articles appearing in newspapers from Asheville to Washington, D.C., and in such magazines and books as *Harper's New Monthly Magazine*, Charles Lanman's *Letters from the Alleghany Mountains*, and Henry Colton's *Mountain Scenery*. Advertisements of the stage line between Morganton and Asheville encouraged travelers to use its route when making a trip to the Black Mountains. Either from Asheville or from the stage stop at

George C. Alexander's, twelve miles to the east, visitors could take hacks to the terminus of vehicular travel at the head of the North Fork valley. Once there, travelers could stay in the "Black Mountain Inn," which was merely an improved version of the cabins built earlier in the decade by Jesse Stepp but then under the management of J. H. Alexander. From the inn, the horse trail could be taken to the illustrious Mountain House, which, following William Patton's death in 1858, had come into the hands of his first cousin, Thomas T. Patton. And for those willing to accept less comfort, a shelter was available on Mt. Mitchell itself. All in all, by the end of the 1850s the Black Mountains had become quite accessible to travelers.

But one aspect of Black Mountain development remains unmentioned. During a three-year period that began in 1858, there emerged the boldest plans yet conceived for the range. During that period no fewer than three movements were initiated to build a turnpike that would enable carriages to travel the full distance to the summit of Mt. Mitchell. These movements were motivated by a desire for profit, a feeling of pride, and demands for an easier means of reaching the highest peak in the range. Not surprisingly, each of the proposed turnpikes had its point of origin in the relatively more developed and accessible county of Buncombe.

The proposition of a turnpike to the Black Mountains was anticipated with great expectation. The excitement and pride with which local residents viewed the proposed culmination of mid-nineteenth-century improvements in the range is perhaps best illustrated by an article published in the *Asheville News* in 1859:

TURNPIKE TO THE TOP OF THE BLACK!

A few years ago it was considered, and not without reason, a proud feat to ascend to the top of the celebrated Black Mountain. We shall never forget the labor it cost us in the spring of 1850. There was nothing in the shape of a road, unless a serpentine trail may be honored with that title. We rode part of the way, walked part, and crawled the remainder.

Things have changed since the time of which we write; and the route to the highest peak . . . has been so much improved that even ladies have passed over the greater portion of it on horseback; and the end is not yet. We publish today a Charter . . . for a TURNPIKE ROAD TO THE HIGHEST PEAK OF THE BLACK MOUNTAIN! Think of that!—Henceforth visitors may drive to that lofty eminence with ease, comfort and perfect safety. No more break neck horseback rides, nor painful foot journeys, but over a smooth and excellent turnpike road you may gain the proud eminence, and look out upon the world beneath your feet. We shall make one more excursion to the Black, if for no other purpose than to enjoy the contrast it will present to our former laborious ascent.

The turnpike charter referred to in this article was one that Thomas T. Patton had submitted to the North Carolina legislature in the fall of 1858. The idea behind the proposal may well have originated with William Patton, who had died a few months earlier. In any case, Judge John L. Bailey, John Burgin, and Montraville Patton, three prominent residents of Buncombe County, were given the responsibility of reviewing and laying off the road.

The route of the proposed turnpike was generally to follow the course of the horse trail that had been built from the North Fork valley to the high peak. The management of the Mountain House had recently been acquired by T. T. Patton, and the route of the turnpike was, not coincidentally, projected to pass by the lodging. As stated in the charter, the road was to be 12 to 16 feet wide, with a grade not to exceed 12½ percent. Once the turnpike was completed to the Mountain House, it was to be opened; and tolls were to be charged to finance construction of the remainder of the road. Charges for use of the road were to be relatively high: $1.50 for road wagons and four-wheel pleasure carriages, $1.00 for other vehicles, and 25 cents for a horse and rider.

Thomas T. Patton was apparently so confident that the turnpike would soon be built that he included the following announcement in an advertisement for the Mountain House that appeared in Henry E. Colton's 1859 travel book *Mountain Scenery*: "A new turnpike road has been lately constructed from Judge Bailey's residence on the Swannanoa, via this House [the Mountain House], to the highest peak. It will afford facilities heretofore unknown to the traveller." But the road was not destined to be completed. Indeed, T. T. Patton's road project apparently never progressed to the construction stage. In 1859 Patton's financial situation took a turn for the worse, and the following year he was obliged to relinquish all his property and interests.

Two other proposals for turnpikes to the Black Mountains were advanced during this period, but they likewise failed to progress very far. One of these proposals, initiated in 1858, was backed by some of the most prominent men in Asheville and Buncombe County— Zebulon Baird Vance, J. W. Woodfin, Nicholas W. Woodfin, John Brigman, Augustus S. Merrimon, and Dr. J. F. E. Hardy. It was to be even more ambitious than Patton's plan, inasmuch as it projected a roadway to begin one mile east of Asheville and to traverse the Great Craggy Mountains and the southern portion of the Black Mountains to Mt. Mitchell (the approximate route followed by the Blue Ridge Parkway). Capital stock in the amount of $6,000 was issued to finance the twenty-five-mile route.

The third turnpike plan, chartered by the North Carolina legislature in 1861, involved the issuance of capital stock in the amount of $10,000. The commissioners named in the charter, most of whom were Buncombe County farmers, hoped to minimize costs by permitting local residents to contribute four days of labor to the construction project, for which the residents would earn free use of the road when it opened.

The backers of the various projected turnpikes to the Black Mountains grossly underestimated the cost and time that such roadways necessitated. A revealing comparison can be made with a similar—and eventually successful—plan to build a turnpike to the summit of New Hampshire's Mt. Washington. The Mt. Washington Turnpike, chartered in 1853, was eight years in the making. After three seasons of construction, the turnpike's capital of $50,000 was exhausted and only half of the road was completed. The average road grade was 12 percent, and the maximum grade was 26 percent—more than twice that which T. T. Patton projected in his plan. A second turnpike company, formed two years later, was successful in completing the Mt. Washington road by 1861.

Even if any of the proposals concerning a turnpike to the Black Mountains had been well formulated and financed, the onset of the Civil War would almost certainly have put an end to such a project. The relatively successful beginning of development in the 1850s, combined with the notoriety that the range acquired during the decade, might well have led to the completion of a turnpike to the summit of Mt. Mitchell by the late 1860s. But the growth and development of the 1850s came to a sudden halt in 1861. The Mountain House and other facilities that had been built for Black Mountain visitors ceased their operations and gradually fell into disrepair. A flourishing era in the history of the Black Mountains had come to an end.

V

The Clingman-Mitchell Controversy: Claim to the High Peak

Not only were the 1850s a decade of development in the Black Mountains, but they also were years of heightened scientific activity. In no other decade, before or since, were the Black Mountains to be the scene of greater advancement, controversy, or tragedy in the name of science. Although it was Arnold Guyot's work in physical geography (to be discussed in Chapter VII) that made the greatest contribution to science, other individuals, including Elisha Mitchell and Thomas L. Clingman, also made contributions. It is with regard to the latter two men that the advancement of science in the Black Mountains took on a new twist.

Much of the popular appeal of the history of the Black Mountains can be attributed to the relationship that existed between Mitchell and Clingman. Although these two prominent North Carolinians had been friends for many years, the controversy in which they became involved during the mid-1850s led to a profound deterioration in their relationship. Over the years various authors have portrayed Mitchell as the protagonist in the dispute and Clingman as the villain—with the protagonist winning in the end. Such a portrayal, however, only disguises the complexities of the controversy. Contrary to popular belief, the Clingman-Mitchell dispute did not involve the question of whether a peak of the Great Smoky Mountains was higher than one in the Black Mountains.[11] Instead, it dealt with the question of whether Elisha Mitchell had indeed been the first person to identify, climb, and measure the highest peak in the Black Mountains.

Unlike Mitchell, Clingman was a native North Carolinian, born in 1812 in the upper piedmont county of Surry. Upon acquiring a classical education, he attended the University of North Carolina in Chapel Hill. Like all students at the university, he took Professor

Thomas Lanier Clingman (1812-1897) was a United States congressman from Asheville at the time of the Clingman-Mitchell controversy. Clingman's scientific inquisitiveness led him into the major dispute with his former college professor, Elisha Mitchell. Photograph of Clingman reproduced from a tintype owned by the late J. Bruce Jarrett, East Bend; used with permission of the Jarrett family.

Mitchell's courses and in so doing undoubtedly acquired firsthand knowledge of the geology and geography of the mountain region. Clingman excelled under Mitchell, as he did in all courses that he took, and he was class valedictorian when he graduated in 1832.

Soon after graduation Clingman became a lawyer, and at the age of twenty-three he was elected to the North Carolina House of Commons. At the end of his term in 1836, he moved to Asheville, which was to be his home for the remainder of his life. The ambitious Clingman soon achieved sufficient recognition and reputation to be elected to the North Carolina Senate. His growing popularity allowed him to move from this position to the United States House of Representatives. With the exception of one term, Clingman served in the House from 1843 to 1858. He then became a United States senator and served in that capacity from 1858 until he resigned in 1861 to take up the cause of the Confederacy. In Congress, Clingman was known for his sagacity, superior powers of analysis, facility in logic, and independence of thought and judgment.

Although not a scientist by profession, Clingman had a strong interest in both the applied and pure aspects of science. Like Mitchell, he advocated the raising of livestock in western North Carolina. But it was in the study of mineralogy that he made his greatest scientific contributions—by locating and/or encouraging the mining of mica, corundum, zircon, platinum, and various gemstones in western North Carolina. Second only to this was his work in topography, for which his name is perpetuated in both Clingman's Dome in the Great Smoky Mountains and Clingman's Peak in the Black Mountain range. In addition, Clingman occasionally made observations on such diverse topics as astronomy, physics, botany, and climatology. According to some critics, his scientific knowledge was shallow; however, his wide interests and insistence on detail, in combination with his political fame, permitted him to correspond with such prominent scientists as Benjamin Silliman,[12] Joseph Henry,[13] Arnold Guyot, and his former professor, Elisha Mitchell.

During the two decades following their years as professor and student at the University of North Carolina, Mitchell and Clingman apparently maintained a friendly and harmonious relationship and occasionally corresponded with one another on subjects of scientific interest. Mitchell described Clingman as a man who "has long taken a deep interest in every thing connected with the mountain region, is well acquainted with the larger part of it, and in whose friendly feeling I could fully rely." In a similar manner, Clingman described Mitchell as a friend whom he "much valued, and my superior vastly in all matters of science." But as the controversy between them grew, their friendship was to erode.

The affinities of Clingman and Mitchell for participating in controversies were about as different as one can imagine. Although it would be an exaggeration to say that Clingman sought out disputes, it is certain that he was more adept and comfortable in handling them. In the political arena, he had on numerous occasions taken the opportunity to engage in spirited discussions and debates. While Mitchell is known to have been involved in three major disputes during his lifetime, he was a more retiring individual than Clingman and was not predisposed toward controversy.

Clingman's differences with Mitchell resulted directly from an excursion the congressman had made to the Black Mountains in 1855. During the previous two decades, Clingman had made several ascents of the range—as much for purposes of recreation as for the pursuit of his scientific interests. Over the years, he became interested in ascertaining which Black Mountain peak was the highest, something he felt Mitchell had never definitely determined. He expressed to friends his belief that the peak presently known as Mt. Mitchell could claim the honor. The primary purpose of his 1855 ascent of the range was to determine whether or not this was the case.

On September 8, 1855, accompanied by several friends, Clingman ascended from the North Fork valley the trail that had been built as far as the high peaks at the southern end of the Black Mountains. The congressman took a barometric measurement while atop the mountain presently known as Clingman's Peak but then known as Mt. Mitchell. (The mountain had acquired the name Mt. Mitchell after either the professor's 1838 or 1844 ascent of the range.) Clingman then continued on, making his way along the height of the ridge to present-day Mt. Mitchell. While atop that peak, Clingman found that his barometer recorded a pressure .19 inches less than it had registered on Clingman's Peak, indicating that Mt. Mitchell had a higher elevation. From Mt. Mitchell, he made sightings of the Black Mountain peaks to his north; and employing the knowledge (acquired from Elisha Mitchell) that Celo Knob and Roan Mountain were several hundred feet lower than the high peaks of the Black Mountains, Clingman became "fully satisfied" that the peak on which he then stood was the highest anywhere in the range.

Clingman's 1855 ascent was not scientifically significant in regard to the barometric measurements he obtained. The elevations he calculated—6,732 feet for Clingman's Peak and 6,941 feet for Mt. Mitchell—were both based on the measurement Mitchell had obtained in the Black Mountains in 1844.[14] Clingman's barometric readings were used only to obtain the difference in elevation between the two peaks, a difference he calculated by using a simplified formula whereby .01 inch of barometric pressure corresponded approximately to 11 feet in elevation. Clingman was aware of the scientific limitations of his barometric work and, in an article written soon after his ascent, remarked that it had not been his intention to prove the absolute height of the high peak; that task, he wrote, should be left to the more competent.

The primary significance of Clingman's 1855 ascent was to indicate which Black Mountain peak was the highest in the range and therefore the highest point east of the Mississippi River. Clingman made this known by providing an accurate and identifiable location for the high peak in a lengthy article he prepared during the month following the ascent. The article was submitted as a letter to Joseph Henry, secretary of the Smithsonian Institution, who in turn asked that it be published in the *Washington City Spectator*. (It was subsequently printed in full in the *Asheville News* and in the *Tenth Annual Report of the Smithsonian Institution*.) In an introduction submitted by Henry to the Washington, D.C., newspaper, the Smithsonian secretary declared:

> The highest point of the Black Mountain [range], now known by the name of "Clingman's Peak," is probably the most elevated point east of the Rocky Mountains.

It appears that as a result of Clingman's 1855 visit to the Black Mountains, the high peak of the range (present-day Mt. Mitchell) had become known locally as Clingman's Peak or Mt. Clingman. Another result of Clingman's ascent was that the newly designated high peak became the common destination point for visitors to the Black Mountains. To facilitate accessibility, the trail that previously had ended at present-day Clingman's Peak (then known as Mt. Mitchell) was extended three miles to the high peak of the range. Clingman's 1855 ascent was thus responsible for the interesting but temporary circumstance of present-day Mt. Mitchell's having been called Clingman's Peak at the same time that present-day Clingman's Peak was called Mt. Mitchell.

The protracted controversy that developed between Clingman and Mitchell can be traced to the article in the *Washington City Spectator*. In the following passage from the article, Clingman issued the somewhat subtle challenge that initiated the dispute:

> But even at the time of [Mitchell's] measurement, I was of the opinion that he had not succeeded in getting upon the highest point of the Black Mountain. In our frequent conversations, both before and since that time, he did not appear to feel at all confident on the subject. It is with reference to the fact that another peak of the mountain is higher than any ascended, or measured by him, that I propose now to speak. . . . When, some twenty years ago, Dr. Mitchell began his observations with reference to the height of the mountain, it was much more

inaccessible, than it has since become, by reason of the progress of the settlements around its base; so that he was liable to be misled, and thwarted by unforeseen obstacles in his efforts to reach particular points of the chain. . . . It has happened that in his several attempts both from the north and the south, he never succeeded in reaching the highest portion of the range.

Thus, the central question of the controversy was raised: Did Mitchell ascend and measure the highest peak in the Black Mountains prior to Clingman's 1855 ascent?

Upon seeing Clingman's article, Mitchell promptly dispatched two letters to Joseph Henry. Although Mitchell paid Clingman several compliments, he nevertheless felt offended by the congressman's statements. He wrote: "My main object in making this communication is to prevent, if I can, the belief that, after having taken so much pains about this mountain, I blundered about the highest peak in it, after all." Mitchell provided Henry with a copy of his unpublished 1835 note (quoted in Chapter III), which gave a running description of the Black Mountain peaks as seen from Yeates Knob. He also included the following description of his 1835 ascent:

On the following day, July 28, I started with two guides. . . . I did not like the course they took, and was not disappointed when I found that they had led me wrong, to a peak too far north, and covered all about its summit with the balsam fir. We could not penetrate farther south that day, and the vacation being just about to close, I was obliged to return to my duties at the University, knowing very well that I had *not* set my foot upon the highest point in the Black Mountain[s].

Mitchell maintained that it was not until 1844 that he reached the highest peak in the range. The description he provided of that ascent was taken almost word for word from the unpublished letter he had written to his wife in 1844 (quoted in Chapter III). He also stated that the peak to which local inhabitants had given the name Mt. Mitchell or Mitchell's Peak had never been "measured, ascended, or even approached nearer than two miles, when he [Mitchell] was once on the southern end of the mountain." This comment, and those pertaining to his 1835 ascent, demonstrate that Mitchell was unable to remember accurately the topography of the range or the details of his various visits. The statement concerning his 1835 ascent directly contradicted his 1835 publication, which asserted that he reached "the Highest Peak of the Black." If, as he said, he did not have time to make an additional ascent of the Black Mountains in 1835, why, then, did Mitchell take the time to reascend Roan Mountain prior to his return to Chapel Hill?

Clingman was undoubtedly disturbed by the contradictory and inexplicable statements that Mitchell had made. He thus wrote to his former professor and suggested that he revisit the range, in order to determine which peaks he had visited during his previous ascents. Clingman also suggested to Mitchell that they refrain from any further discussion of the Black Mountains until the professor had had that opportunity. Although the congressman seems to have expected the controversy to continue, he told Mitchell that he was "extremely averse" to such a discussion with a former preceptor and a highly valued friend.

The controversy continued, with both participants writing letters either to each other or to Joseph Henry. In his letters Clingman expressed the belief that Mitchell had ascended a peak at the head of Cattail Fork during his final 1835 ascent.[15] Whether independently or influenced by Clingman, Mitchell also came to believe that "the guides took me to a point near the head of the Cat-tail fork." Curiously, Mitchell did not have a copy of his 1835 *Raleigh Register* article when the controversy began; however, even when he did acquire one in February, 1856, he still expressed the belief that he had not reached the high peak of the Black Mountains in 1835. Mitchell did believe, however, that he had correctly sighted the high peak while on Yeates Knob in 1835. As for his 1844 trip, the professor continued to maintain, as he did throughout the dispute, that he had ascended and measured the high peak on that occasion. Clingman, on the other hand, believed that Mitchell's description of the route of ascent and the natural features present on the summit indicated that the peak he ascended in 1844 was Mt. Gibbes. Clingman's argument concerning the route of ascent was one of the most convincing of the controversy.

During the summer of 1856 the dispute became public, with Mitchell submitting his articles for publication in the *Asheville Spectator* and Clingman submitting his to the *Asheville News*. At the same time, the personal animosity between Mitchell and Clingman increased considerably. Referring to the original article the congressman had published concerning the controversy, Mitchell stated:

My own name is mentioned there and it is represented that in my measurements of the mountain, I failed to discover and ascend the highest peak. This is a total mistake of Mr. Clingman's. . . . If his errors are permitted to stand, they will have the effect of throwing the heights that have been ascertained around this mountain into inextricable confusion, and may bring all the measurements made by me into discredit. It may therefore be expected, with some reason, that I shall state what the facts really are.

Mitchell continued by presenting the relatively strong argument that he had correctly sighted the high peak of the range from Yeates Knob in 1835. As to whether he ever actually reached this peak, however, the professor made only some vague and inconsistent statements. Although Mitchell still believed that the peak he had ascended in 1835 was at the head of Cattail Fork, he now admitted that at the time of his ascent he thought he had reached the range's highest peak. He justified his change of opinion by stating that "at the distance of 21 years one is liable to mix up and confound the impressions of one ascent with those of another." The professor also now admitted that in 1838 he ascended "what have since been called Mts. Gibbes and Mitchell [present-day Clingman's Peak], one or both, and took an observation." Somewhat surprisingly, Mitchell said that he had not been aware that the latter peak had been so commonly regarded as the highest in the range.

During July, 1856, Mitchell used a portion of his summer vacation to make a hasty trip to the Black Mountains. He regretted the time that the controversy was taking up, but he nonetheless felt that he needed to return to the range to clear up points of concern both in his own mind and in the minds of others. Secondarily, he made the trip to improve his earlier calculations of elevations in the range by means of a new barometer he had acquired.

On his way to the Black Mountains, Mitchell met another scientist headed for the range: Arnold Guyot. Guyot, a professor of physical geography at Princeton University, was making an extended study of the Appalachian chain of mountains. However, because Mitchell had only a short time to spend in the range, he left Guyot after they had arrived in the North Fork valley. Then, accompanied by Frederic

The Mt. Gibbes-Clingman's Peak-Potato Knob complex (*right to left*) was ascended by Elisha Mitchell in 1856. Prior to attaining its present name in the late 1800s, Clingman's Peak was called Mt. Mitchell, a name that probably evolved from an earlier ascent of the peak by Mitchell. During the early 1850s Clingman's Peak served as the destination point for visitors who ascended the Black Mountains from the North Fork valley. Photograph (1976) by the author.

Burnett, who had guided him during his 1838 trip, Mitchell ascended the Black Mountains by way of the trail that had been constructed to the high peak. Although he presumably took some barometric measurements, they were never made public. Concerning this ascent, Mitchell stated: "I have . . . spent in this instance about as much time [on the range's] . . . top, as in all my former visits put together; nearly a whole day." While on Mt. Gibbes, Burnett told Mitchell that that was as far as they had gone in 1838. Although Mitchell wanted to contact some of his former guides in Yancey County, time did not permit him to do so, and he returned to Chapel Hill with little accomplished.

In a pamphlet issued soon after returning from the Black Mountains, Mitchell admitted that he had made some incorrect assumptions concerning the topography of the range. He nevertheless continued to insist that he had reached the high peak in 1844, implying that he had not done so in 1835. Based on the form and appearance of present-day Clingman's Peak and Mt. Gibbes, he concluded that neither one of those peaks was the one he had ascended in 1844.

Until late in 1856, Clingman, to support his own position, had relied heavily upon statements made by Mitchell. Because Mitchell had made quite a few contradictory or vague statements, the congressman had a number of remarks from which to choose when presenting his side of the controversy. In Mitchell's August, 1856, pamphlet, the professor gave the following defense of the variety of statements he had made:

> But he [Clingman] says that my own different accounts of the high peak, do not agree with each other, nor with the peak itself, and that there are errors in my statements of what occurred in connexion [sic] with the first measurements of the mountain. Nothing is more probable. . . . I saw the high peak times enough to fix its position, and the course to be pursued in reaching it, tolerably well; but was less to be trusted at any considerable distance of time with regard to its appearance.

Mitchell also expressed the need for still another trip to the Black Mountains.

The hostility between Mitchell and Clingman came to a head in the professor's August, 1856, pamphlet. In response to a pamphlet issued by Clingman during the previous month, Mitchell made a personal attack on the congressman that appears to have been largely unjustified. The professor offered the following advice to Clingman:

> Do not, sir, issue another foolish and detestable pamphlet. It will do me some injury, but greater mischief to your own character, not only as a politician, but also as a man; especially when I take up the pen, and expose its untruth, its injustice, its weakness, and its wickedness. You put an instrument of torture into the hands of your enemies, of every name, with which they may annoy you to any extent. . . .

57

The words, "old friend," do not harmonize with the malignity that character-
izes the latter part of your pamphlet. It is likely to be said in view of the whole,
that you do not know what friendship is; that whatever you may claim to feel of
that kind, is hollow and pretended, or, if real, is unreliable and worthless, snap-
ping asunder, whenever there is a slight opposition of interest.

While Clingman's desire to make known the truth appears to have
been stronger than his bond of friendship, he apparently never suffered attacks from his political enemies on account of the quarrel
with Mitchell.

During the fall of 1856, for the first time during the dispute,
Clingman introduced direct evidence from one of Mitchell's guides.
The testimony of William Riddle, Mitchell's guide in 1844, dealt a
severe blow to the professor's already shaky case:

Mr. William Riddle states that many years ago, he thinks in 1844, he went with
Prof. Mitchell to the top of the Black Mountain— that they went from his house
on Caney River, by way of the Green ponds, and there took up a ridge [Spruce
Pine Mountain Ridge] to a place called the beach [sic] nursery, and from thence
turned to the right and went in a southerly direction as direct a course as possible
to that part of the [Black] Mountain since called Mount Gibbes, near Mount
Mitchell [present-day Clingman's Peak]. . . . He says further that he knows the
point of the mountain well, which has since been called Clingman's Peak
[present-day Mt. Mitchell], and that he never did go on it with Prof. Mitchell. He
says further that if he had intended to have gone on it, he would have kept up
the ridge from the beach nursery, and on reaching the top of the Black he would
have turned to the left hand to get on the highest point. . . .

Riddle's statement agrees substantially with the statements Mitchell
himself made concerning the route of ascent (see Chapter III for the
statement made by Mitchell in 1844). The difference was that Riddle
thought the route led to Mt. Gibbes, while Mitchell thought it led in a
different direction—to the highest point in the range, present-day Mt.
Mitchell.

Using his analytical abilities and logic, Clingman attacked Mitchell with
an analogy illustrative of the professor's position concerning his 1844
ascent:

Suppose that a person not a resident of our State should say that he had visited
Chapel Hill in the year 1854, and that he had gone there directly in a railroad car
from Weldon and had stopped at Guion's Hotel, situated on the public square
near the State House. Upon his being told that he had probably mistaken
Raleigh for Chapel Hill, as his description harmonised with the former place and
not the latter, he asserts with great vehemence that it was Chapel Hill that he
had gone to, because the Legislature was then in session and that he had
attended there the debates in the two houses. . . . On being assured that all these
statements went to prove that he was not at Chapel Hill but must have been at
Raleigh, he becomes transported with rage, denounces those who doubt as "fool-
ish," "detestable," "wicked," "dishonest," and affirms that he did go to Chapel
Hill for that he was accompanied by A. B. and C. D. These persons on being

called upon say that they accompanied him to Raleigh but never to Chapel Hill, and that they cannot be mistaken about it, as they were residents of Raleigh and knew the localities well. In a case like this what weight would be attached to such a man's assertions, even if he accompanied them with all the abusive epithets in the language?

In the autumn of 1856 the controversy entered a period of quiescence, with Mitchell on the defensive. When the dispute was renewed in the summer of 1857, it would take a major shift of direction and include an increased number of participants.

VI

Tragedy in the Black Mountains

As noted in the previous chapter, Mitchell's visit in 1856 to the Black Mountains left several matters unresolved, and the professor felt that another trip to the range was necessary. The trip he made to the range in 1857 had two major purposes. First was his desire to clear up some of the questions pertaining to the Clingman-Mitchell controversy by ascertaining as best he could which Black Mountain peaks he had ascended during previous trips. To this end, he wanted to obtain statements from his earlier guides and also to reacquaint himself with the topography of the range. He probably also wished to reascend Yeates Knob and refresh his memory of the high peaks of the range as seen from that location in 1835.

A second motive behind Mitchell's 1857 trip was to make an accurate determination of the elevation of the high peak by means of a survey method known as leveling. This was a slow and painstaking process in which a level, a device similar to a spyglass, was employed to sight a point on the landscape perfectly horizontal with one's eyes. The surveyor would then advance to the point thus sighted and continue the process. The number of such sightings between the beginning point of survey and its end multiplied by the distance between the surveyor's feet and his eye level would yield the difference in elevation between the two points. In addition to his desire to measure accurately the elevation of the high peak, Mitchell hoped to compare the accuracy of barometric measurements with those obtained by leveling.

In early to mid-June, 1857, the professor left Chapel Hill for the North Carolina mountains. He was accompanied by his thirty-one-year-old daughter, Margaret; his eighteen-year-old son, Charles; and a servant boy named William. After making a very brief stop in Asheville, Mitchell proceeded to the Black Mountains and established his headquarters at Jesse Stepp's lodging at the head of the North Fork valley. Beginning at the lower end of the valley, he spent between one and two weeks leveling up to the elevation of the Mountain House. On Saturday, June 27, while at the apparently unopened lodge, the professor penned the following letter to his wife:

Patton's Mountain House, Saturday Morning
Some day in June 1857

My Dear Mary

I have your letter enclosing the checks. We are here two thirds of the way from the base of the mountain to the top. Charles and myself with William keeping batchelor's hall, getting on very well—in excellent health—living mostly on corn bread and bacon. . . .

Yours affectionately,

E. Mitchell

That same day, at about 2:30 P.M., Mitchell left Charles and William at the Mountain House and set off on foot for the settled portion of the upper Cane River valley, about ten miles distant. Although he told no one the exact purpose of his trip, it seems certain that he wanted to contact some of his former guides for information concerning his previous ascents and perhaps make arrangements for reascending Yeates Knob. He may also have desired to preach to the local inhabitants the following day. Prior to his departure, Mitchell instructed his son to descend the mountain to Stepp's, where his sister was staying. Charles was to meet his father back at the Mountain House on the following Monday.

Future governor Z. B. Vance, who happened to be visiting the Black Mountains at the time, recounted what then happened:

On Monday his son repaired to the Mountain House to meet his father, but he did not come. Tuesday the same thing occurred, and though considerable uneasiness was felt for his safety, yet there were so many ways to account for his delay that it was scarcely thought necessary to alarm the neighborhood; but when Wednesday night came and brought no token of him, his son and Mr. John Stepp immediately started on Thursday morning to Caney River in search of him. On arriving at Mr. Thos. Wilson's, what was their astonishment and dismay to learn that he had neither been seen nor heard of in that settlement! They immediately returned to Mr. Stepp's, the alarm was given, and before sundown Friday evening [July 3] companies of the hardy mountaineers from the North Fork of Swannanoa were on their way up the mountain.

On Saturday, July 4, a week after Mitchell had left Charles and William, two search parties, one each from the North Fork and Cane River valleys, began combing the mountains. Within two days, their numbers had more than doubled to sixty persons. News that the professor was missing caused citizens from Asheville and other locations to leave their jobs and join in the search. The Buncombe men were led by Jesse Stepp, Fred Burnett, and Eldridge Burnett, all of whom

Zebulon Baird Vance (1830-1894), a native of Buncombe County, was a friend of the Mitchell family and a political opponent of T. L. Clingman. An acknowledged leader, he helped direct the search for Elisha Mitchell in 1857. Five years later he became North Carolina's Civil War governor. Photograph of Vance from Clement Dowd, *Life of Zebulon B. Vance* (Charlotte: Observer Printing and Publishing House, 1897), facing p. 104.

were North Fork inhabitants well acquainted with the Black Mountains. Z. B. Vance, although not well versed in woodcraft, also stood out as a leader of the Buncombe group. The somewhat smaller Yancey contingent was led by Thomas (Big Tom) Wilson (1823-1908), a local settler and mountain guide who had lived for several years at the head of the Cane River valley near the Green Ponds.

For three days the Buncombe and Yancey men divided into squads and fruitlessly searched the ridges, slopes, and watercourses of the Black Mountains. They found only a few signs, and these were located relatively close to the Mountain House. By the following Monday, few searchers had any hope that Mitchell might be found alive. This, combined with the physical strain of passing through mazes of interlocking rhododendron growth, caused some men to want to give up the search and wait a few days for buzzards to circle over the body. Such a thought naturally upset Mitchell's son, who had been actively engaged in the search. Most of the men, it appears, decided to continue looking.

Convinced that the search by the Buncombe men in the southern portion of the range would continue to be fruitless, Big Tom Wilson and four other Yancey inhabitants decided to look for "signs" in the vicinity of the high peak. On the morning of Tuesday, July 7, about one quarter mile west of the peak, Adoniram D. Allen, a son of Mitchell's 1835 guide (having the same first name), spotted an impression in the moss. Several in the party believed it to be a bear's track, but Big Tom concurred with Allen that it was the footprint of a man. Big Tom argued that a bear would have kept to rocky ledges, where it could not be trailed or followed, but a man would naturally have

Thomas D. (Big Tom) Wilson (1823-1908) was the leader of the Yancey County contingent of the search party that sought Elisha Mitchell in 1857. During the late 1800s Big Tom gained considerable fame as a guide in the Black Mountains. From original photograph in the possession of the North Carolina Museum of History, Raleigh; reproduced by permission.

walked where it was easiest to do so. A short distance away, the party found another sign. This time it was the broken trunk of a small balsam, with a footprint stretched across it. Its size convinced Big Tom that it could only be the print of a man. About 200 yards further away, an additional sign appeared—one that dispelled the doubts of everyone in the group. Looking at an impression on the root of a balsam tree, Big Tom asked: "Did you ever see a bear's heel with tacks in it?"

Certain that they had found Mitchell's trail, Big Tom's search party returned to the high peak and sent word to the Buncombe searchers at the southern end of the mountain. Although various accounts of the search differ somewhat, it appears that two of the Yancey searchers then left for the Cane River and two Buncombe searchers joined the group. The search party now consisted of Big Tom Wilson, Adoniram D. Allen, Jim Allen, Calvin Patton, and a Mr. Burgin.

Once again setting out on their mission, the searchers continued to follow the newfound tracks down a ridge known as Little Piney. If the tracks were indeed those of Mitchell, the professor had gone past the newly blazed trail from the Cane River valley to the high peak and had instead taken a route that approximated the one he is believed to have taken during his 1835 ascent. About halfway down the mountain, the professor's tracks turned off Little Piney ridge. Instead of dropping off the ridge on its southern slope, as he had done in 1835, he had descended on its northern side, taking a more direct course toward the settled portion of the Cane River valley. The search party followed Mitchell's tracks down to the creek at the base of the northern slope of the ridge. There the tracks led directly down the creek bed, through its pools and across the logs that had fallen into it. It was speculated that anyone taking such a route would have done so only if darkness had overtaken him. On following the creek for a short distance, Big Tom apprised his fellow searchers of his belief that they might find Mitchell at the base of a waterfall just ahead. In the following passage, Big Tom related what happened on his reaching the top of the falls:

I looked down and could see nothing, so I turned to the right and went down the mountain [slope] to the lower end of the pool, where a mountain birch log had fallen across it. I walked out on the log and saw his [Mitchell's] hat, and called to the boys. Then I walked across the log and around upon a rock on the left side of the falls (facing down stream,) and underneath a pine log that had fallen over the falls, I saw his body, and called to the boys, "Here he is. Poor old fellow." "Have you found him?" they called back, and I repeated that I had.

Mitchell could be seen several feet below the surface of a 15-foot-deep pool, his body prevented from rising to the surface by the large snag that had fallen into the water. Attempting to reconstruct the circumstances of the accident, Big Tom noticed some displaced moss on the rocky ledge on the fall's north side and surmised that the professor had been attempting to make his way around the falls when he slipped and fell into the pool below. Because only a slight bruise was found on Mitchell's forehead, it was the general opinion of those who

Mitchell Falls, located about halfway up the west slope of Mt. Mitchell, was the site of Elisha Mitchell's death in 1857. The 40-foot-high waterfall has carved out a 15-foot-deep pool at its base. Photograph (1975) by the author.

64

gathered at the scene of the accident that the professor had been stunned to unconsciousness by his fall and then drowned. A watch found in the unfortunate man's pocket had stopped at 8:19, from which it was surmised that the time of the accident was shortly after darkness on Saturday, June 27, the day he had departed from his son. As unusual and unlikely as it may seem, the place where Mitchell met his death was only one or two miles distant from the location about which he had written thirteen years earlier: "what a comfortable place it would be to die in."

While arrangements for the removal and interment of the body were being made, it was kept preserved in the cold water at the base of the waterfall. During this time approximately fifty people from Yancey County gathered at the falls, which became known as Mitchell's Falls, and they decided that the most appropriate place for burying the body was atop the high peak. After the body was viewed by the coroner, a litter was constructed by wrapping the body with cloth sewn together over a long wooden pole. The ascent to the high peak would have been difficult even without such a load, since the vegetation was dense and the elevation rose 2,300 feet in just over two miles. By taking turns, however, the Yancey men were able to make the climb in less than four hours. Atop the peak, they met a large group of citizens from Buncombe County who had brought with them a coffin to be used in conveying the body to Asheville. Big Tom and the Yancey men felt that since they had found the body, they had the right to decide where it should be buried. A fight nearly ensued between the Buncombe and Yancey men, but Z. B. Vance called Big Tom aside and explained that it was the wish of Mitchell's daughter, Margaret, that the body be taken to Asheville. Without further challenge, the Buncombe men proceeded to convey the body down to the North Fork valley and on to Asheville.

In a gesture of respect and love for the deceased professor, a large number of citizens met the body outside Asheville; and as the procession approached town, court was adjourned, houses of business closed, and church bells tolled. The body was taken to the Presbyterian church, where a moving funeral sermon was delivered. There, on July 10, 1857, Professor Mitchell's remains were interred in the small graveyard beside the church.

Mitchell's death and the circumstances surrounding it excited much attention throughout North Carolina. Even the *Asheville News*, which had taken Clingman's side during the controversy with the professor, declared that "No individual calamity ever produced so great and painful a shock in this community." To many, Mitchell "died a martyr to science and scientific knowledge," as stated by the *Asheville Spectator*. As news of the tragic death spread throughout the state, public meetings were held in several communities and resolutions

After being examined by the county coroner, Elisha Mitchell's body was carried up the steep slopes of the Black Mountains by Yancey County men. Artist's conception of the recovery of Mitchell's body by Kenneth Whitsett, from Fred M. Burnett, *This Was My Valley* (Ridgecrest: By the author, 1960), [p. 103].

At the request of Elisha Mitchell's daughter, the professor's body was carried to Asheville, where a funeral and burial ensued at the First Presbyterian Church. The churchyard in which Mitchell was buried lies beneath the present church building. The following year Mitchell's body was reburied on the Black Mountain peak that was to acquire his name. Photograph (1978) by the author.

concerning the deceased were passed by both public and private organizations. It is doubtful that there was a newspaper in the state that did not carry at least one article about Mitchell's death. Although the professor's reputation was primarily within the state, some outside newspapers, including the *National Intelligencer* (Washington, D.C.) and the *New York Times*, carried notices of his death.

The story of Mitchell's death did not end with his burial in Asheville, however. North Carolinians, particularly those in Buncombe and Yancey counties, felt that Mitchell should be buried at some point along the height of the Black Mountains. Even the Buncombe men who had conveyed the professor's body to Asheville thought his permanent resting place should be atop the range. Such a feeling, it appears, resulted from Mitchell's having died a martyr to science and from his being the first person to claim the Black Mountains as the highest in the eastern United States. The wishes of the public were fulfilled when, a few days after Mitchell's burial in Asheville, the professor's wife received news of his death and consented to allow his body to be reburied atop the range. Without any public objection from Clingman or his supporters in the controversy, and undoubtedly with the encouragement of Mitchell's supporters, it was decided that the appropriate place to bury the professor was atop the high peak of the range.

For reasons not completely known, it was not until June of the following year that the body was exhumed and reinterred on the high peak. On June 15, 1858, Mitchell's coffin was taken by wagon from Asheville to Jesse Stepp's at the upper end of the North Fork valley. The trail to the high peak had been improved in advance of the reinterment, and transporting the body was easier than it had been the previous year. Nevertheless, after carrying the coffin on an oxen-drawn sleigh for the first two miles, it became necessary to carry it by hand over much of the remaining distance to the Mountain House. Not until darkness had set in did the body and its escorts reach the lodge.

The following morning the coffin was taken on the sleigh to the high peak. Atop the peak, those who bore the body joined others who had gathered there for the occasion. Approximately two hundred people were present—members of the family, graduates of the University of North Carolina, and local inhabitants of Buncombe and Yancey counties. At twelve o'clock noon, the Right Reverend James H. Otey, Episcopal bishop of Tennessee and a former student and instructor at the University of North Carolina, delivered a funeral sermon. Following the bishop's address, David L. Swain, then president of the university, delivered a final eulogy to the professor. Mitchell's body was then laid to rest in a shallow grave on the rocky summit.

A plan to erect a $5,000 monument to Professor Mitchell had been initiated during the previous year by a group of Buncombe County men, but the ambitious plan failed to gain a sufficient number of subscribers. For the next thirty years, Mitchell's gravesite was marked only by a large pile of rocks. In 1888, with money furnished by the family, a monument to the professor's memory was placed on the high peak. Shaped like an Egyptian obelisk, it stood 12 feet tall and consisted of white bronze surrounding a hollow interior. The monument served as a focal point of interest for many visitors to the Black Mountains. However, overzealous tourists weakened it considerably by chipping off pieces of bronze for souvenirs, and in 1915 it was destroyed, apparently the victim of a windstorm. The sarcophagus that stands on the summit at the present time was erected at the request of the North Carolina Historical Society in 1926.

Contrary to what might have been expected, the Clingman-Mitchell controversy did not end with the professor's death. Supporters of Mitchell, who undoubtedly were aware that Clingman had gained considerable ground against their friend, defended the professor's position with even greater zeal than Mitchell himself had done. Led by Professor Charles Phillips (one of Mitchell's colleagues at the university), Z. B. Vance (one of Mitchell's friends and former students), and David L. Swain, they hoped to make use of the sympathy generated by the professor's death to further their cause. Beginning with the obituary notices prepared on Mitchell, the professor's proponents submitted to the *National Intelligencer* and a number of North Caro-

It was not until 1888—thirty-one years after Elisha Mitchell's death—that a monument honoring him was placed on the summit of Mt. Mitchell. The bronze monument, pictured here, served as a focal point for tourists to the high peak until it was destroyed in 1915. Photograph from an early postcard (ca. 1910) held by North Carolina Collection, Pack Memorial Public Library.

lina newspapers a series of articles that attempted to further his cause. In their desire to strengthen Mitchell's scientific reputation and to perpetuate his memory in the Black Mountains (as well as to express a measure of suppressed anti-Clingman sentiment), they advanced a number of arguments that were either invalid or of questionable validity.

However, in one of their arguments that does appear to be valid, Mitchell's proponents took a major departure from the professor's position during the controversy. Contrary to what Mitchell had maintained both at the time of his 1844 ascent and for the duration of the controversy, his defenders asserted that he had reached the high peak of the range during his final 1835 ascent. Although they did not dispute Mitchell's allegation that he had also reached the high peak in 1844, they focused their attention on his 1835 ascent. In so doing, they provided strong support for the contention that the professor had indeed ascended and measured the range's high peak prior to Clingman's 1855 ascent.

Although Clingman did reply to these initial articles, he offered no challenge[16] to the final pro-Mitchell article, published in March, 1858. In this article Mitchell's proponents presented the full testimony of

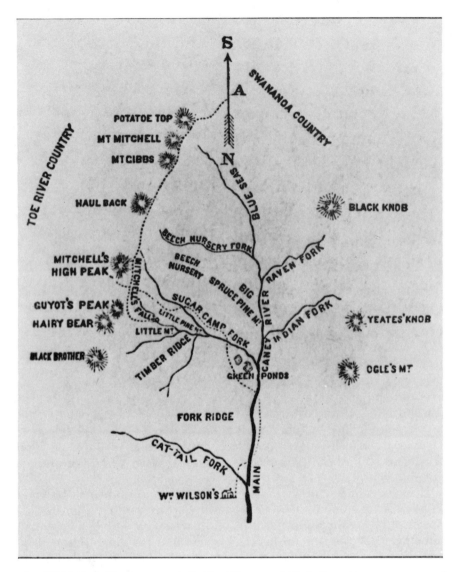

In 1858 Mitchell's proponents in the Clingman-Mitchell controversy prepared this map of the Black Mountains and the Cane River valley, which shows the route of Mitchell's final 1835 ascent of the range as described by William Wilson and the route Mitchell traveled in 1857 from the Mountain House (A) to the site of his death. The nomenclature used on the map came from three sources: Arnold Guyot, Nehemiah Blackstock, and Big Tom Wilson. "Mitchell's High Peak" is present-day Mt. Mitchell, and "Mt. Mitchell" is present-day Clingman's Peak. Map from E. S. J. Bell and others (eds.), "Dr. Mitchell's Investigations among the Mountains of Yancey County," *North Carolina University Magazine*, VII (March, 1858), p. 301.

William Wilson, who had served as one of the professor's guides during his final 1835 ascent. Wilson's statement concerning the route of ascent indicated that Mitchell had indeed reached the high peak of the range in 1835. Wilson said that from the Green Ponds, he, Adoniram Allen, and the professor had gone up Sugarcamp Fork and then ascended Little Piney Mountain to the peak at the height of that ridge. (The testimony is presented more fully in Chapter III.) In addition to obtaining Wilson's declaration, Mitchell's proponents asked Wilson to retrace the route he had taken with Mitchell in 1835; he did so and attested that the peak they reached—present-day Mt. Mitchell—was the one Mitchell had ascended and measured in 1835. It is ironic that the man who provided the strongest support for Mitchell's case was a guide whose name the professor had been unable to remember.

Considerable evidence supports the validity of Wilson's claim. Clingman had, in 1857, obtained a statement from Wilson that was very similar in content to the one given to Mitchell's proponents. The fact that these statements are in close agreement indicates not only that Wilson was consistent in the accounts he gave but also that neither the congressman nor Mitchell's supporters distorted the guide's statement. Adoniram Allen was not alive to corroborate Wilson's declaration. However, Nathaniel Allen, his son, testified (to Mitchell's proponents) that he had often heard his father describe the route of the ascent and that his own familiarity with the range made him certain that the peak ascended by his father and Mitchell was the one that had recently become known as the highest peak. Aside from such testimony, it seems unlikely that a resident of the upper Cane River valley would not have been able to lead Mitchell directly across the valley to the peak that he had selected as the highest while on Yeates Knob just one day earlier.

Summarizing the findings of the controversy, it appears that, directly contrary to what Mitchell maintained during the dispute, he did reach the highest peak of the Black Mountains during his trip of 1835 but not during the trip of 1844. The place names and descriptions given by the professor and his guide, William Riddle, for their 1844 trip indicate that the peak ascended on that occasion was not present-day Mt. Mitchell but was instead a portion of the Mt. Gibbes-Clingman's Peak-Potato Knob complex. There is, however, strong evidence that Mitchell did correctly point out which peak of the range was the highest while viewing it from Yeates Knob in 1835. Furthermore, if the testimony of one of his guides is to be trusted—and it appears that it can—then Mitchell did indeed reach the high peak of the range in 1835.

That peak began to acquire Mitchell's name in 1858, although it was not so much from evidence adduced by the controversy as it was from the circumstances of Mitchell's death and burial. Indeed, the permanent affixation of the name Mt. Mitchell to the high peak was probably the most significant consequence of the professor's death. Beginning in the summer of 1857, Mitchell's friends in the dispute had begun a movement to change the name of the high peak from Clingman's Peak to Mt. Mitchell. During the reinterment on the peak in 1858, both Bishop Otey and David L. Swain proclaimed the justness of calling the high peak by the professor's name. Otey implored:

Here then, and to-day . . . in the name of truth, honor, and justice; by right of prior discovery; by merit of being the first to claim the honor of actual measurement and mathematical determination; by virtue of labors endured with unremitting patience, and terminated only by death; we consecrate this mountain by the name of MT. MITCHELL and we call upon you to speak your approval and say Amen!

Members of the crowd that had gathered on the high peak voiced their hearty approval.

Even without the prompting of Otey and Swain, the fact that Mitchell was buried on the high peak, combined with the fading of the Clingman-Mitchell controversy, made it increasingly difficult to refer to the mountain by any other name. It was only a matter of time before the highest peak in the eastern United States became universally known as Mt. Mitchell. Ironically, the "Mt. Mitchell" at the southern end of the Black Mountains—the mountain whose height T. L. Clingman had demonstrated to be inferior to the high peak—was to acquire permanently the name Clingman's Peak toward the end of the century.

VII

Arnold Guyot: Geographer Unrivaled

Although not as emotionally stirring as the Clingman-Mitchell controversy and Elisha Mitchell's martyrly death, Arnold Guyot's work in the Black Mountains during the late 1850s was of considerably greater scientific significance. Indeed, from the standpoint of accuracy and thoroughness, no other nineteenth-century scientist made a greater scientific contribution in the Black Mountains than did Guyot. Although André Michaux's reputation as a scientist rivals that of Guyot, Michaux's work in the Black Mountains was lacking in thoroughness. Within the field of geography, Mitchell's investigations had been pioneering—but they were not definitive. In contrast, Guyot's work in physical geography—both in the Black Mountains and throughout the Appalachian chain—was so accurate and thorough that it was not only unprecedented but also came to be regarded as a standard accepted for many decades.

Unlike Mitchell, Guyot was not a native of America. Born in 1807, Guyot spent his childhood in Switzerland and then traveled to Germany for his higher education. First studying to be a clergyman, Guyot, because of his scientific inquisitiveness, changed his vocational direction and in 1835 became one of the first students to earn a doctorate in science. In contrast to Mitchell, Guyot concentrated his efforts in a particular field—physical geography. That, combined with his intelligence and zeal for work, enabled him to make outstanding scientific contributions. In the Alps, he conducted important studies on glaciation; and he helped to set up a uniform system of weather stations throughout Switzerland. For almost a decade he served as professor of physical geography at the university in his home city of Neuchatel.

Following the lead of his friend and colleague, Louis Agassiz,[17] Guyot emigrated to the United States in 1848. In 1854 he became professor of physical geography and geology at Princeton University, where he eventually directed the first American graduate work in geography. During his three decades in the United States, he demonstrated that he had an interest in teaching not only college-level students but also much younger pupils, and for the latter he prepared an innovative and widely adopted series of school geographies, maps, and map-drawing cards. Unlike many of his colleagues, he emphasized the use of field studies and maps over textual readings.

Guyot established a scientific reputation soon after arriving in America. In 1848 he met Joseph Henry and from him obtained support to set up guidelines and design the instrumentation for a national meteorological observation system similar to the one he had developed in Switzerland. He provided initial direction for the project by establishing fifty weather stations at widely diverse localities throughout New York and Massachusetts. The United States Signal Service, the predecessor of the National Weather Service, eventually evolved from Guyot's meteorological work.

Guyot made significant improvements to the barometer, which not only benefited his meterological work but also improved the accuracy of another major focus of his scientific work, the measuring of mountain elevations. Motivated by the limited and widely varying sources of information then in existence, Guyot took upon himself the monumental task of describing, mapping, and barometrically measuring the entire Appalachian mountain system. Few major mountains escaped Guyot's notice. In total, he made more than 12,000 barometric observations at hundreds, if not thousands, of different locations.

Arnold Guyot (1807-1884), a Swiss-born physical geographer, spent a decade investigating the Appalachian chain of mountains. He spent several summers in the Black Mountains, one of the two ranges to which he devoted his greatest attention. From a photograph made in 1867; supplied by the author.

Beginning in 1849, just one year after he arrived in America, Guyot spent several years working in the northern Appalachians. There he focused on the highest group, the White Mountains. He then shifted his attention southward, and after spending a few years in the relatively low central Appalachians, he concentrated his efforts on what he called the culminating portion of the entire system, the southern Appalachians.

In the South, as elsewhere in the chain, Guyot attempted to provide a better picture of the general structure of the mountains, basins, and valleys located there. He performed trigonometric surveys to fix the locations of landmarks in relation to each other; these surveys enabled Guyot, along with his assistant, Ernest Sandoz, to map accurately the entire Appalachian system with detailed inserts for two of its culminating ranges—the White Mountains of New Hampshire and the Black Mountains of North Carolina. The map was first published in Switzerland in 1860 and was republished the following year in the *American Journal of Science and Arts* along with an article in which Guyot summarized the results of his Appalachian studies. While Guyot's written descriptions of the geographic structure of the Black Mountains did little to improve on those previously given by Mitchell and Clingman, his map did represent the first detailed and accurate graphic portrayal of the range and its surroundings.

Guyot's work in measuring elevations not only helped to perfect the barometric method but also provided some definitive information on the relative and absolute heights of Appalachian peaks. Guyot hoped to determine once and for all which peak was the highest in the East. Not only was Mt. Washington still being put forward for the honor, but in 1858 a peak in the Great Smoky Mountains measured by T. L. Clingman, S. B. Buckley, and Joseph LeConte had entered the running.

Although Guyot spent considerable time in the Great Smokies, he concentrated the greatest portion of his work in the southern Appalachians on what he believed to be the region's highest range—the Black Mountains. His goals were to make sense out of the confusion that had developed as a result of the Clingman-Mitchell controversy and to determine accurately the relative heights of the various peaks in the range. Of the four summers he spent in the South, portions of at least three were given to work in the Black Mountain range. In 1856, the year he met Elisha Mitchell, Guyot spent a month traversing the full length of the range, carefully measuring at least fourteen of its points. In 1858 and 1859 he spent a major portion of his time remeasuring those points as well as measuring new localities. In the

This close-up of a map of the Black Mountains was produced by Ernest Sandoz under the direction of Arnold Guyot in 1860. The elevations indicated are those measured by Guyot in the late 1850s. Guyot called present-day Mt. Mitchell "Black Dome," perhaps to avoid showing partiality concerning the Clingman-Mitchell controversy. Guyot's "Mt. Mitchell" is present-day Clingman's Peak. Map from Arnold Guyot, "On the Appalachian Mountain System," *American Journal of Science and Arts*, Second Series, 31 (March, 1861); photograph courtesy North Carolina Collection, Pack Memorial Public Library.

Black Mountains, as in the Great Smokies, Guyot's concern for accuracy motivated him to spend a night on each of the highest peaks of the range in order to observe minor changes in barometric readings.

Because of his skill and persistence, Guyot's elevation measurements in the Black Mountains and elsewhere achieved an unprecedented accuracy and consistency. While both Mitchell's and Clingman's measurements in the North Carolina mountains had often been in error by several hundred feet, Guyot's determinations were incorrect by no more than 30 feet (as compared to the most recent measurements available). Interestingly, Guyot believed that his measurements were even more accurate. Such confidence can be attributed in part to the fact that the calculations he made in different years were very similar to each other. But perhaps more important, the accuracy of his measurements was supported by the work of James C. Turner, an engineer with the North Carolina Railroad, who in 1857 painstakingly leveled from the North Fork valley to Mt.

Mitchell and found the height of the peak to be only 4 feet higher than Guyot had determined it to be.

In addition to obtaining more accurate absolute elevations for more than twenty localities in the Black Mountains, Guyot appears to have determined correctly the relative elevations of the range's highest points. After Mt. Mitchell, to which he assigned an elevation of 6,707 feet, he ranked the high peaks as follows: Mt. Craig, 6,671 feet; Balsam Cone, 6,619 feet; Cattail Peak, 6,611 feet; Big Tom, 6,610 feet; Mt. Gibbes, 6,591 feet; and Clingman's Peak, 6,582 feet. With the elevations of these peaks differing by only a few feet, the difficulty Elisha Mitchell experienced in determining which point was the highest can be appreciated.

Although some individuals undoubtedly took considerable interest in the scientific work occurring in the Black Mountains, many must have felt that concentrating such effort on the measurement of mountains was a bit nonsensical. The following passage from an 1857 issue of *Harper's New Monthly Magazine* humorously speaks of such scientific efforts, alluding not only to Guyot's work but also to that of Mitchell and Clingman. Speaking to a friend, a fanciful visitor to the Black Mountains comments:

> It is impossible to tell by the eye . . . which of these great peaks is the highest; and it must have been a source of deep mortification to the Balsam Cone when Guyot's barometer decided the question and gave the crown of pre-eminence to the Lord of the Black Dome.[18] We may even now trace upon each gloomy front the jealousy and hate of approved superiority. They doubtless talk of it among themselves . . . [and] it would not be difficult to imagine what they say.
>
> The Balsam Cone whispers to the Cat Tail, "Harkye, princely brother. Do you believe these confounded *savans* can measure so neatly with their instruments as to tell whether he or I is the taller? I once held myself above him."
>
> "Ah!" groans the Black Brother,[19] "I was once at least his equal; but he has been so puffed up with his cursed pride, I fear he overtops us now in reality. Since Mitchell measured him he has grown three hundred feet from pure conceit."
>
> "Hist, brothers!" says the Cat Tail, slyly, "we are too boisterous. Now do you know I have long doubted whether it was really he the Professor measured, but have good reason to believe it was one of us—myself, perhaps."
>
> "You?" exclaims the Cone, contemptuously looking down . . . on the conceited speaker.
>
> "Or perhaps it was you," suggests the Cat Tail; "but after all, what mighty difference does ninety-two feet make? Does he think we are valleys for that? . . . If . . . we could keep it before the people that he was the wrong mountain, nobody would be the wiser, and one of us might be king."

Frivolity aside, it cannot be denied that Arnold Guyot brought geographic knowledge of the Black Mountains to a level that it had never before attained. Through his barometric and trigonometric work, he provided a surprisingly accurate written and graphic description of the range. His corresponding work in the Great Smoky Mountains and elsewhere proved that Mt. Mitchell, the Black Mountain peak he called Black Dome, was the high point of the Appalachian chain. Guyot was careful to avoid the use of the names "Clingman" or "Mitchell" to designate the high peak, but he did not hesitate to comment on the respective scientific contributions of the two men. Of Clingman, Guyot said that "we are indebted for the first clear, accurate, and most graphic description of the Black Mountain[s]." He similarly praised Mitchell, describing him as a "noble scientific pioneer" in the field of mountain measuring but adding that because of "unfavorable circumstances and the want of proper instruments," the Chapel Hill professor was not certain of which points of the range he had measured. Although the names Mitchell and Clingman have become permanently etched in Black Mountain nomenclature, Arnold Guyot, the man who did the most to elucidate the geography of the range, is memorialized only elsewhere.[20]

Probably because of Guyot's thoroughness, relatively little geographic work has been performed in the Black Mountains since the 1850s. Not surprisingly, the highest peak has received the greatest attention. Although the United States Coast and Geodetic Survey obtained a measurement of 6,688 feet for the altitude of Mt. Mitchell in the late 1870s, the calculations made by Guyot and Turner in the 1850s continued to be the most commonly accepted figures until after the turn of the century. Finally, in 1930, the United States Geological Survey ran a series of levels to Mt. Mitchell and obtained the measurement accepted at the present time—6,684 feet. The precise elevations of other Black Mountain peaks have yet to be determined.

Both from a scientific and developmental point of view, the decade of the 1850s was a golden era in the history of the Black Mountains. At the beginning of the decade, the range had been little explored. Yet, just ten years later, geographic knowledge of the range had become well refined and toll roads to its summit were being planned. With regard to this heightened geographic knowledge and increased visitor access, the quest for the East's highest mountains had been realized. But other quests remained. In the 1850s there was only a hint that the range would undergo exploitation. But exploitation did occur, eventually fostering a movement to preserve the natural heritage of the Black Mountains. These two themes—exploitation and preservation—would dominate the history of the range during the ensuing 100 years.

VIII

Exploitation and Preservation

The onset of the Civil War brought a virtual halt to the activities of scientists and tourists in the Black Mountain range. The economy of the South did slowly recover, and with that recovery tourists gradually began to seek the range in increasing numbers. Scientists, too, began making their way back to the Black Mountains. While some of their findings were quite significant, there was no single period in which scientific activity attained the fervor or notoriety it achieved during the golden era of the 1850s.

Along with government mapmakers and surveyors who refined the geographic knowledge of the Black Mountains, climatologists, botanists, and zoologists sought to increase man's knowledge of the range. Perhaps spurred by the interests of Arnold Guyot, a weather station was established on Mt. Mitchell in 1873; but it was soon destroyed by fire, and more continuous weather observations were not made until the twentieth century. Botany, which in the late 1700s had become the first science to be studied in the range, was largely neglected until 1925, when John H. Davis, Jr.,[21] began a six-year study delineating the plant communities found in the Black Mountains.

In contrast to botany, zoology had received very little attention in the Black Mountains or elsewhere in the southern Appalachians prior to the Civil War. Just four years after the war, Edward Drinker Cope, an eminent paleontologist, made the first significant zoological reconnaissance in the Black Mountains. Based on his fieldwork, Cope published in the *American Naturalist* an article detailing his belief that much of the animal life in North Carolina's mountains was the same as that found 500 or 1,000 miles to the north in New England and southern Canada. More extensive ornithological studies made by William Brewster and John Simpson Cairns in the Black Mountains during the 1880s and 1890s proved that Cope's belief concerning "northern" affinities was correct. Brewster, a zoologist at the Boston

A very short lived weather station was erected on the summit of Mt. Mitchell in 1873 in an effort to obtain data from high-elevation localities. Engraving from Edward King, "Among the Mountains of Western North Carolina," p. 541.

Society of Natural History, was very impressed by the faunal zones he observed in the Black Mountains, noting that the zones were the most sharply and clearly defined that he had ever seen. Cairns, unlike Brewster, was a local resident (from Weaverville, Buncombe County), and he was able to make frequent observation and collecting forays to the range.

As fate would have it, the relationship between tragedy and the pursuit of science in the Black Mountains did not end with Elisha Mitchell's death. On June 10, 1895, J. S. Cairns, at the age of thirty-three, accidentally shot himself while collecting bird specimens in the range. Cairns had been traveling alone, and a search party was formed by one of the men who found Mitchell's body thirty-eight years earlier—the now well-known mountain guide Big Tom Wilson. Within less than a day of searching, Cairns's body was found near a trail just north of Balsam Gap. Unlike Mitchell, Cairns was relatively unknown, and his death went largely unnoticed.

The Civil War and the hard times of Reconstruction had an even greater impact on tourism in the Black Mountains. The Mountain House, with no one to care for it, gradually fell into ruin during the quarter-century following the war. No facility of comparable quality

Less than forty years after Elisha Mitchell's death, another scientific investigator, John Simpson Cairns (1862-1895) accidentally lost his life in the Black Mountains while engaged in the pursuit of science. As with Mitchell, Cairns's body was found by Big Tom Wilson. Photograph of Cairns courtesy Museum of Comparative Zoology, Harvard University.

took its place until after the turn of the century. Small cabins were occasionally built on Mt. Mitchell itself, but they were unmanaged and never lasted more than a few years, the victims of fires or vandalism. Accommodations at the base of the range in the North Fork and Cane river valleys were simple and rustic. At the head of the North Fork valley, William Glass and "Widow" Patton (no relation to William Patton) provided lodging to visitors during the 1870s and 1880s. George C. Alexander's, located at the mouth of the North Fork along the main east-west road from the North Carolina piedmont to Asheville, was the closest high-quality lodging establishment to the Black Mountains.

Because of the depressed economy and the lack of good visitor facilities, relatively few travelers sought out the range during the years following the Civil War. The number of travelers undoubtedly increased with the completion of the Western North Carolina Railroad to the vicinity of Asheville in 1880, but tourism in the Black Mountains does not appear to have reattained the popularity it enjoyed during the 1850s. Visitors to the range came from throughout the eastern United States seeking good scenery, cool weather, mountain sunrises and sunsets, unusual plants and animals, Elisha Mitchell's grave and the site of his death, and, last but not least, the highest peak in the East. A round-trip excursion from either the North Fork or Cane river valley continued to be a two-day journey made on foot, horseback, or by mule. Visitors often hired the services of a guide, most notably Big Tom Wilson in the Cane River valley or William Glass in the North Fork valley. Climbers used the two main trails that had been built during the 1850s, and most went all the way to Mt. Mitchell. Once there, they either stayed in a makeshift cabin, if present, or camped under a large shelving rock near the summit that was sometimes dubbed the "Black Mountain Hotel."

Until the late 1800s the Black Mountains existed largely in a wilderness state. No major alteration of the landscape had occurred. Although cattle were permitted to graze at the higher elevations, none of the fine grazing farms that Elisha Mitchell had envisioned existed atop the range. Perhaps the most significant influence of man upon the environment was that increased settlement, hunting, and the desire to protect one's family were beginning to reduce the populations of some animal species in the area.[22] The relative absence of exploitation of natural resources was not to last, however. Soon after the Civil War, the bounty of the range began to be pursued.

Exploitation of natural resources in the Black Mountains first came in the form of mining. Although interest in the mineral resources of the range had been stimulated as early as the 1840s by Thomas L. Clingman, it was not until 1869 that Garrett Ray opened the first mine in the range. This mine, as well as several others that were developed in the Black Mountains, was located in the vicinity of Celo Knob, at the northern end of the range. Another, known as the Cattail Branch Mine (discovered in 1906), was situated at an elevation of 5,500 feet.

Mica (both biotite and muscovite) was the major mineral mined in the Black Mountains during the late nineteenth and early twentieth centuries, but beryl, tourmaline, garnet, zircon, feldspar, kaolin, cyanite, albite, quartz, flourite, apatite, and rutile were also extracted to varying degrees. Over the years, mines opened and closed according to fluctuations in demand. The Ray Mica Mine was an exception, however, in that it operated continuously until the 1940s. Mica from the Ray mine won a prize at the 1873 world's fair in Vienna. From the standpoint of both quality and size, mica from the vicinity of the Black Mountains was said to be unequaled in the world. The mica industry of the Black Mountain region suffered a severe blow during the 1940s as a result of the federal government's acquisition of much of the land and the withdrawal of a government subsidy. The latest known mining operations in the Black Mountains continued until about 1970 on the northern flank of Celo Knob. While no mining currently occurs in the range, it remains an important part of the economies of Yancey and several other western North Carolina counties.[23]

The environmental damage in the Black Mountains caused by mining was small when compared to the destruction resulting from the extensive logging operations that denuded much of the range in the early 1900s. Beginning in 1912 and continuing for about a decade, hundreds of men were involved in the removal and processing of spruce, balsam, and hardwood timber from the slopes of the Black Mountains. The exploitation began on the Buncombe side of the range with the purchase of the timber rights to 9,000 acres of land on the southern and eastern flanks of the Black Mountains. Originally acquired by C. A. Dickey and J. C. Campbell, the timber rights were sold in 1913 to Fred A. Perley and W. H. Crockett, prominent lumbermen from Williamsport, Pennsylvania.

The first order of business for the lumbermen was to begin building a logging railroad to be employed in removing the timber from the mountains. Because of the steepness of the terrain, the general public was astonished by the plan to build a railroad to the upper slopes of the range. No insurmountable problems ensued, however, and after being surveyed by C. A. Dodd, the railroad was successfully constructed under the supervision of George Meyers and E. L. Sutton. From its lower terminus in the Swannanoa valley one mile east of the town of Black Mountain,[24] the railroad climbed 3,500 feet over a distance of approximately twenty-one miles. The railroad was given a grade of only 5½ percent, especially remarkable since only three trestles and nine switchbacks were needed. In contrast to the projected toll roads of the 1850s was the rapidity with which the railroad was constructed; just one year after work began in 1911, the first trainload of logs was hauled out of the mountains over the continually extending railroad. By 1913 eighteen miles of track had been laid, and the railroad reached the slopes of Clingman's Peak. By 1914 it reached the 5,800-foot contour just one-half mile below the summit of Mt. Mitchell. From this location, near what was to become known as Camp Alice, the railroad was extended eastward along the eastern flank of the range to Celo Knob and westward across Stepp's Gap to the vicinity of Balsam Gap. Because spruce and balsam were the primary targets of the logging operations, much of the railroad track was built along the 5,800-foot contour near the lower limit of the spruce-fir forest.

At its lower terminus just east of the town of Black Mountain, the railroad joined with the Southern Railway (formerly the Western North Carolina Railroad). At that juncture a large double band mill, capable of turning out 110,000 board feet (fifty carloads) of lumber daily, was constructed. Completed in 1912, the mill was a large, roofed structure that was open on its sides. Logs delivered to the mill by the Perley and Crockett Railroad were thrown off the railcars into a man-made lake built at the mill. From there, those logs more than 8 inches in diameter were drawn up by a track leading into the mill, where they were cut into lumber. The finished lumber was then carried on a short spur line to the standard-gauge Southern Railway

For a decade the Perley and Crockett lumber mill transformed logs brought out of the Black Mountains into lumber and pulpwood. The mill was located just east of the town of Black Mountain, which had been named for the range towering above it. Photograph (ca. 1915) by William A. Barnhill; from Barnhill Collection, Pack Memorial Public Library.

tracks, where it was placed on cars most often bound for the Northeast. Much of the lumber was used in constructing houses and furniture; during World War I, however, a large portion of the spruce was diverted into the manufacture of airplanes. Logs smaller than 8 inches in diameter were cut up for pulpwood and sent to Champion Fiber Company in Canton, North Carolina, for processing.

George Meyers and J. W. Sturgill were given charge of the lumber camps that were established in the Black Mountains. In the summer of 1913 two hundred men were at work in the forest, cutting, loading, and hauling timber to the mill. Most of the men were natives of the Carolinas, Tennessee, or Virginia, although a contingent of twenty-five men were Austrian. Before the First World War 3 forty-two-ton Climax engines, 2 thirty-six-ton Shay engines, 2 loaders, 2 steam skidders, and 70 logging cars were being used to take timber from the Black Mountains. Among the logging camps established by 1915 were one below Clingman's Peak and one at Commissary Ridge a mile southeast of Mt. Mitchell. The lumber camps usually contained quarters, a cookhouse, and a commissary for the loggers. At the beginning of the logging operations, it was estimated that there were 250 million board feet of timber on Dickey and Campbell's

9,000-acre tract and that it would take about ten or twelve years to haul all the timber to the mill. As it turned out, this estimate was quite accurate, for logging operations on the tract continued until 1921.

Meanwhile, at the upper end of the Cane River valley in Yancey County, two lumber companies had acquired the timber rights to more than 18,000 acres. The Carolina Spruce Company, begun by Charles K. Perry of Philadelphia and headquartered in the Yancey County village of Pensacola, laid seventeen miles of rail line on the company's 5,200-acre tract in the Black Mountains. The Brown Brothers Lumber Company, officially called the Murchison Lumber Company, was headquartered in Eskota, three miles south of Pensacola. On their 13,000-acre tract (the Murchison Boundary), Ned and Ward Brown, also from Pennsylvania, laid twelve miles of rail line. The spruce timber from their acreage was apparently sold to Perley and Crockett, and the latter company transported it out of the range on its railroad. Both of the Yancey-based lumber companies used the tracks of the Black Mountain Railroad, which had been built between 1907 and 1913 from Kona on the Clinchfield Railroad[25] through Yancey's timber and mining districts to the southern end of the Cane River valley at Eskota.

As on the Buncombe side of the range, the boom years for the Yancey-based logging operations were during World War I. The need for labor during this time was critical, and about four hundred Italians and Austrians—the first outsiders ever seen by many Yancey County families—were brought into the Cane River valley. The hub of the logging business and excitement was at Pensacola, where the offices and main commissary of the Carolina Spruce Company were located. The commissary included a post office, a complete department store, a grocery store, a hardware store, a seed and feed store, a barbershop, and a drugstore complete with soda fountain. For entertainment, a circus went to Pensacola annually, and movies were shown every Friday and Saturday night in a makeshift theater. Still more excitement came to the now-tranquil valley in 1916 when a movie entitled *Then I'll Come Back to You*, starring Alice Brady and Jack Sherrill, was filmed at the site of the Carolina Spruce band mill and log pond. After World War I, logging of the Black Mountains in Yancey County continued at a decreased rate until the Black Mountain Railroad tracks between Eskota and Burnsville were taken up in 1933.

Between 1913 and 1915 logging activity in the range was rapidly expanding, and a few outspoken individuals voiced their alarm at the denuding of the area's forests in the name of progress. In August, 1913, the *Asheville Citizen* made the following comments:

From a standpoint of commercialism, the wonderful activity of this district, felling these great monarchs of the forest, cutting them into short lengths, transporting them to the mill, cutting them into lumber, distributing them in the various building channels, affords a scene of intense interest and thrills the being with a sense of development and progress, turning nature's resources into money—the man-created standard of values.

Think of it! Within another twelve months the magnificent forests of spruce and balsam on the slopes of Mt. Mitchell, the highest point east of the Rockies, 6,711 feet and the pride of the entire eastern section of the United States[,] will fall before the axe of the lumberman to be turned into money!

Such statements were an appeal to the sentiments and pride of North Carolinians, and indeed in the absence of such appeals it is doubtful that the movement to save Mt. Mitchell from the lumberman would have been successful. Foremost among those whose sentiments were aroused by the denuding of Mt. Mitchell's forest cover was Locke Craig, governor of North Carolina from 1913 to 1917. Craig, a resident of Buncombe County since 1883, had spent a good deal of time in the North Fork valley over the years and had regularly made trips to the Black Mountains and Mt. Mitchell. Like others, Craig considered Mt. Mitchell and the surrounding forest to be a sacred place—one not to be destroyed by the hand of man. In an address before the North Carolina Forestry Association in January, 1915, he declared:

It was on a place like this [Mt. Mitchell] that Moses communed with God, Who revealed Himself to man. He has given this sacred place to us, and we should do our best to preserve it. *North Carolina should protect it, and own it for herself and for her citizens forever.*

Craig described to the association an event that had occurred during the preceding July—an event that initiated his campaign for the preservation of the forest surrounding Mt. Mitchell:

Last year I was invited up to celebrate the opening of the twenty mile logging railroad from Black Mountain station to [the vicinity of] Mount Mitchell as a great enterprise. But when I looked all around, where I had been bear hunting as a boy, and saw this vast desolation all below, I told them they had gotten the wrong man to come up and celebrate the opening of their railroad. I felt like a man that stood amidst the ruins of his home after the conflagration had destroyed it.

Craig told the forestry association that lumbermen were destroying North Carolina and that they had every legal right to do so. He said that if North Carolinians wanted to save the Mt. Mitchell area, they would need to take up the cause themselves. In the meantime, at Craig's request, Perley and Crockett agreed not to cut the timber on a 4-acre tract at the summit of the mountain.

Perhaps the most eloquent plea for preserving the forest surrounding Mt. Mitchell was expressed in a poem written in 1914 by George

Locke Craig (1860-1925), using his influence as North Carolina's governor, became a powerful force behind the movement to establish Mt. Mitchell State Park. Photograph of Craig (1915) from North Carolina Collection, Pack Memorial Public Library; supplied by the author.

Tayloe Winston, former president of the University of North Carolina:

> From out the primal sea I rose on high,
> Above the clouds I kissed the sunlit sky,
> My rock the oldest in this rock-built earth:
> When I was born, it was the great world's birth.
> Long million years my crumbling sides did yield,
> To rain and frost and wind, a fertile field
> For widening Piedmont plain and ocean shore.
> Now nature kind assails my life no more;
> At last in verdure soft and warm I'm clad,
> Mid sapphire skies my emerald peaks are glad,
> But hark! what frightful terror, new and dire!
> 'Tis human greed for gold! 'tis axe and fire!
> O mighty State, prevent this deed of shame,
> This great dishonor keep from thy great name!

Others, too, spurred by civic pride and deeply felt sentiments, voiced their opinions concerning the Mt. Mitchell area. In addition to the pride North Carolinians felt in their state as home of the highest peak in the East, several individuals and groups, including Governor Craig, wanted to preserve Mt. Mitchell because of the interesting history associated with it. These people emphasized that the peak was the location of the death and grave of Elisha Mitchell, one of North Carolina's most distinguished men. To destroy the forests on this Black Mountain peak, they argued, would dishonor the memory of the professor.

87

Several local inhabitants were also active in the movement to save Mt. Mitchell, among them Chase P. Ambler, Neptune Buckner, and Charles A. Webb, all of Asheville, and E. Frank Watson of Burnsville. Although most were motivated by civic pride and their regard for nature, Buckner, who was secretary of the Asheville Board of Trade (now the Chamber of Commerce), also appeared to have been influenced by economic considerations. The logging activity that so drastically affected the scenic beauty of the Mt. Mitchell area had the potential for influencing the developing tourist industry in the region, particularly in Buncombe County.

There also existed scientific arguments that provided additional strength to the movement to save the Mt. Mitchell area. State forester J. S. Holmes, the North Carolina Forestry Association, and other individuals and groups were especially concerned about the effects of fires that followed the logging. The fires were most often of two types: those that were purposely set by the logging companies to clear off highly flammable slash (debris) from their landholdings, and those that were ignited accidentally, most often from sparks from railroad engines. In either case a consuming fire was often the result. These fires were of such intensity that they not only destroyed all vegetation in an area but also burned the soil to depths of up to one foot. This destruction of the soil and the seed source made it highly unlikely that natural reforestation of the spruce-fir forest would take place. And as J. S. Holmes stated in 1911, the artificial reforestation of spruce would not likely be undertaken by lumber companies because of the expense of the operation and the uncertainty of the results. Other major concerns relating to the logging activity were its effects on water quality, through the washing of soil into the streams and rivers, and on water quantity, which would increase, making floods more likely because of the decreased capacity of the deforested land to absorb water.

The state or federal government was seen as the means by which Mt. Mitchell could be saved from the lumbermen. As interest in the movement mounted, the North Carolina Forestry Association, the Asheville Board of Trade, and other organizations adopted resolutions setting forth in detail their support for such action. The first such resolution, adopted in 1913 by the North Carolina Forestry Association, urged the North Carolina legislature "to pass a bill to make a State park and demonstration forest area including the top of Mount Mitchell." At least partially because of the novelty of a movement for land preservation, a bill introduced in the North Carolina legislature in 1913 failed to be enacted. However, the support of organizations and individuals, especially that of Governor Craig, continued to mount, and in 1915 a second bill was submitted

Logging operations in the Black Mountains made the forest more susceptible to fire. The damaging fires that occurred gave growing concern to those who desired to protect the Mt. Mitchell area from further destruction. Photograph from Raymond Pulliam, "Destroying Mt. Mitchell," *American Forestry*, XXI (February, 1915), p. 89.

to the state legislature. This bill was introduced in the state Senate by Zebulon Weaver of Buncombe and in the state House of Representatives by G. P. Deyton of Yancey. It moved quickly through the legislature, passing both houses by large majorities, and was ratified into law on March 3, 1915. The law set forth the procedure by which a state park including the summit of Mt. Mitchell was to be established.

The state park founded by this bill was possibly the first of its kind—state or federal—to be established in the South. Ignoring the sentimental reasons that were so dominant in the movement to create the park, the authors of the preamble to the 1915 bill emphasized scientific and concrete reasons why the state of North Carolina should acquire a portion of Mt. Mitchell for a state park.

Whereas, the summit of Mount Mitchell in Yancey County is the greatest altitude east of the Rocky Mountains; and whereas, the headwaters of many of the important streams of the State are at or near the said summit and the forest is being cleared which tends to damage and injure the streams flowing through the said State from the mountains to the Atlantic ocean; and whereas, it is deemed desirable that this beautiful and elevated spot shall be acquired and permanently dedicated as a State park for the use of the people of the entire State seeking health and recreation; and, whereas, unless the said land is acquired by the State at this time, the cost of acquiring it at a later date will be greatly increased and the water courses may be damaged and the beauty of the scenery destroyed by removing the growth therefrom, and irreparable damage accrue . . .

As directed by the 1915 act, the governor appointed a commission of "five practical business men"[26] to acquire, or if necessary condemn, land to be contained within the state park. The act instructed the commission to buy as much land as it could for the sum of $20,000. A survey was conducted, and it was decided that the state park should occupy a long, narrow tract comprising the land one quarter mile on each side of the Black Mountain ridgeline from (Mt.) Big Tom (located 1½ miles north of Mt. Mitchell) to Stepp's Gap. Through a complex series of land transactions involving six parties, including all three lumber companies, the commission purchased 525 acres of land in 1916 for about $13,400. Of this amount, $10,500 went to Perley and Crockett for their timber rights. More than half of the eastern portion of the 525-acre tract had already been logged, and in 1917 two fires from Perley and Crockett's operations penetrated the park, destroying much of the timbered southwestern portion of the tract. In 1918 the commission acquired an additional 700 acres without standing timber, extending the park boundary northward to Cattail Peak and westward down to the railroad grade at about 5,800 feet. Smaller acquisitions in 1935, 1962, and 1969 expanded the park to its present size of 1,469 acres.

In appreciation of Governor Locke Craig's efforts in the preservation of Mt. Mitchell, the highest peak of the Black Brothers[27]—and

Windfalls are presently a dominant feature near the crest of the Black Mountains. Many of them appear to owe their existence to the logging operations of the early twentieth century. Logging and the resulting fires exposed the uncut forest to the full force of strong winter winds that occur frequently at the high elevations, beginning the windfall process. Windfalls were gradually pushed upslope until they reached the height of a ridge. These three photographs were taken from Mt. Mitchell looking north along the Black Mountain crest. The top photo, made about 1915, shows the area prior to logging operations and the presence of a windfall. The center photo, made in 1954, and the bottom view, made in 1978, show the upslope progression of a lengthy windfall. Photographs supplied by the author.

the second-highest point in the eastern United States (elevation, 6,647 feet)—was named Mt. Craig. The new name, approved by the United States Board on Geographic Names in 1947, apparently resulted from the fact that in the mid-1940s this peak and not Clingman's Dome in the Great Smoky Mountains was identified as the second highest in the East. At the same time, the lower Black Brothers peak was officially named Big Tom after the mountain guide Thomas D. Wilson.

The logging operations of the twentieth century left only a small portion of timber in the Black Mountains untouched. But to a considerable degree the land did recover, and spruce and fir trees once again took hold—although possibly in lesser numbers—on the higher slopes of the range. Some areas, such as the vicinity of Camp Alice and the Black Mountain ridgeline south of Celo Knob, did not revert to forest but instead acquired a meadowlike growth of grasses and herbs. Windfalls, scarcely known before the logging operations, began to occur in earnest on the upper slopes of the range, and they continue to be a prominent feature of the landscape. The federal government began its efforts to reclaim the land in the mid-1910s, when it began purchasing the cutover land on the eastern slope of the range south of Celo Knob. In the late 1920s Perley and Crockett helped to reforest the area by contributing more than 100,000 seedlings of Fraser's fir, red spruce, and an introduced species, Norway spruce.

The logging operations of the early twentieth century proved to be the greatest threat the Black Mountains had experienced. But out of this threat to the range's integrity, a state park was established and a new era of tourism was ushered in.

IX

The Return of Tourism

The renewal of tourism that began in the Black Mountains in 1915 was not nearly so much a result of the establishment of the state park as it was of the logging operations in the range. Even before the notion of a state park became a realistic possibility, Fred A. Perley and W. H. Crockett had made plans to operate passenger trains on the logging railroad they had built. Although they had no intention of discontinuing the use of their railroad for logging operations, they were convinced by the great interest expressed by tourists and developers to operate passenger trains from the lower terminus of the railroad a mile east of the town of Black Mountain to the point that became known as Camp Alice, a mile below the summit of Mt. Mitchell.

As early as 1913 Perley and Crockett were using their railroad to carry special groups of visitors from the Swannanoa valley to the heights of the Black Mountains. By the following year, the logging company had built two or three passenger cars at their mill, and the railroad was opened to individuals and groups on a limited basis. The experimental operations conducted during these two years convinced Perley and Crockett that an expanded passenger railroad could be a successful financial venture that would not interfere significantly with their logging business.

To carry out the details of an expanded passenger service, Perley and Crockett hired Colonel Sandford H. Cohen to serve as general passenger agent and promoter of the railroad. Cohen was an ideal choice for this position in that he had previously gained experience in the promotion of tourism as manager of the Greater Western North Carolina Association, an organization that promoted tourism in western North Carolina, and as the developer of the Isle of Palms resort in South Carolina. Indeed, more than any other person, Cohen was responsible for launching the new era of tourism that began in the Black Mountains at this time.

The trip to Mt. Mitchell by way of Perley and Crockett's logging railroad proved to be a very popular tourist attraction. For the first time, the heights of the Black Mountains could be reached with considerable ease and quickness. Photograph (ca. 1915) from Barnhill Collection, Pack Memorial Public Library.

Tourists from throughout the southeastern United States were attracted by Cohen's formal efforts and by word-of-mouth advertising to experience the trip on the "Mount Mitchell Railroad." Pamphlets were printed, souvenir booklets sold, and full-page advertisements printed in the *Asheville Citizen*. Indicative of the zest with which Cohen undertook his duties is the following excerpt from a promotional pamphlet on the railroad:

The World's Greatest Scenic Mountain Trip
MOUNT MITCHELL
Altitude 6,711 Feet
The Top of Eastern America

Over the Mount Mitchell Railroad, The Scenic Marvel,
The Road of Mountain Magnificence, Going to The Crest
of The Land of the Sky, Above the Clouds, The Trip
Presents a Perfect Panorama of Unsurpassed Magnificence,
Grandeur, Beauty and Sublimity, Unequaled on the Globe.

Despite the devastation caused by the logging operations then occurring in the Black Mountains, a writer for the *Citizen* remarked that many who had visited Switzerland and the Rockies felt that "there is no mountain scenic trip in the world that surpasses the trip to Mount

Mitchell." A more realistic assessment is that the Mt. Mitchell Railroad provided what was perhaps the most interesting and novel travel experience in the South. (A comparable passenger railroad had been completed up the slopes of New Hampshire's Mt. Washington almost a half century earlier.)

Although hundreds of visitors had already traveled on the Mt. Mitchell Railroad, it was not until July, 1915, that the road was formally opened to passenger traffic. A promotional trip made by a large gathering of newspaper editors from throughout the Carolinas preceded the official opening on July 16. At first only two trips a week were offered to tourists, but in August the number of trips was doubled. During that month the early success of the passenger railroad prompted Fairfax Harrison, president of the Southern Railway, to construct "Mt. Mitchell Station" at the junction of the two railroads just east of the town of Black Mountain. A convenient connection schedule was established with the Southern Railway to Asheville, enabling visitors to Mt. Mitchell to spend their nights at a wide variety of accommodations in the rapidly growing mountain metropolis.[28]

Travelers desiring to ascend the Black Mountains boarded passenger cars at Mt. Mitchell Station, within sight of the Perley and Crockett lumber mill. At this station, visitors were able to make connections for Asheville via the Southern Railway. Photograph (ca. 1915) from Barnhill Collection, Pack Memorial Public Library.

Depending on the weather, the Mt. Mitchell Railroad utilized as many as seven passenger cars to carry a maximum of 250 people to Camp Alice on each run. On each trip, the train carried a conductor, an engineer, a fireman, and two or three brakemen. The train departed Mt. Mitchell Station at 9:40 A.M. and required three hours to travel the approximately twenty-one miles to Camp Alice. For reasons of safety, the return trip took three and one half hours, with the train arriving at Mt. Mitchell Station at 6:47 P.M. The cost of the round trip from Mt. Mitchell Station to Camp Alice was $2.50, half of what it had been during the railroad's experimental operations the previous year. To provide for interest and orientation along the route, identifying signs were placed at more than twenty locations; and to keep passengers refreshed and entertained, drinks, candy, souvenir booklets, and personal photographs were available.

The ease and quickness with which visitors could reach the highest peak in the East, combined with Sandford Cohen's intensive advertising campaign, made the 1915 season the first in which several thousand visitors attained Mt. Mitchell's summit. Not since the 1850s, when William Patton's Mountain House attracted visitors to the Black Mountains, had a tourist enterprise in the range been so successful. Cohen's efforts were rewarded still further in 1916 when the Mt. Mitchell Railroad conveyed more than 10,000 visitors to Camp Alice between mid-May and mid-October. In one week alone, almost 1,600 tourists made the trip. Although Cohen originally believed that it would be possible to operate the passenger railroad nine months a year, he must nevertheless have been quite pleased at the business generated by the railroad during the five months in which it did operate.

Camp Alice, the terminus of the rail line for passengers, apparently was constructed for the tourist trade by Perley and Crockett, either in 1914 or 1915. The camp consisted of a large rustic dining hall and several platform tents for those who desired to spend the night on the mountain. The dining hall not only served hot, family-style food to the limited number of overnight visitors but also prepared a lunch for the large masses of people who daily ascended the mountain on the passenger railroad. The interior of the dining hall, described as "very rough," featured unfinished planks for paneling and enough long, unfinished tables and benches to accommodate 250 people. Relatively little interaction occurred between the passenger railroad tourists and the Perley and Crockett loggers, whose headquarters and commissary at that time were at a place that subsequently became known as Commissary Ridge. The operation of Camp Alice was leased to H. Russel Cohen, who is believed to have been a nephew of Sandford Cohen. The camp was named for a daughter or daughter-

96

Camp Alice was the upper terminus for passengers traveling the Mt. Mitchell Railroad. In its early days the camp consisted of a large rustic dining hall and a few tents to accommodate overnight visitors. Photograph (ca. 1915) by William A. Barnhill; from Barnhill Collection, Pack Memorial Public Library.

in-law of the elder Cohen, who, interestingly enough, took no part in the facility's operations.

After the tourists on the passenger railroad ate lunch at Camp Alice, most took a moderate one-mile hike to Mt. Mitchell's summit. The wide, well-graded trail that led them there was probably built by Perley and Crockett. Atop the mountain, visitors could view their surroundings from the relatively open summit or from a sturdy wooden tower constructed by Perley and Crockett in 1915 or 1916. Two cabins located near the summit were available for use by visitors who desired to spend the night on the mountain.

Like visitors of today, most tourists of the early 1900s went to Mt. Mitchell to view the scenery and to be able to say that they had been atop the highest peak in the eastern United States. Unlike today, however, many early twentieth-century tourists took a deep interest in the story of Elisha Mitchell, and seeing his grave on the summit was a significant aspect of their visits.

Within but a year or two of its opening, Perley and Crockett's passenger railroad to Camp Alice had become one of the most popular tourist destinations in the eastern United States. The longevity of the

97

This early observation tower atop Mt. Mitchell was constructed by Perley and Crockett in 1915 or 1916. It could be reached from Camp Alice by means of a mile-long trail. Photograph (ca. 1915) by William A. Barnhill; from Barnhill Collection, Pack Memorial Public Library.

tourist enterprise, however, cannot be touted. After only four years of full operation, Perley and Crockett announced in June, 1919, that passenger service would be halted so that their railroad line could be used solely for the removal of timber. This announcement dismayed the Asheville Board of Trade, whose success at promoting the passenger service likely contributed to its ultimate demise. Without the railroad, the operation of Camp Alice was also halted.

With the closing of the Mt. Mitchell passenger railroad, there ensued a strong demand for an easy means of access to the high peak. Many pressed for the reopening of the railroad, but this was not to be. The railroad, however, was replaced by another means of access, by which even more tourists would ascend to the heights of the Black Mountains. In 1922, just one year after Perley and Crockett terminated their logging of the range and four years after the passenger railroad ended its operations, the Mt. Mitchell Motor Road began carrying its first automobile passengers to the high peak.

Not coincidentally, the operation of the Mt. Mitchell Motor Road was in many respects similar to that of the passenger railroad that preceded it. Both were essentially Buncombe phenomena, with each of the initiators and operators of the motor road having played a major role in the railroad. Fred A. Perley was president of the Mt. Mitchell Development Company, which operated the motor road, and C. A. Dickey, one of the partners who had built the railroad, was its secretary. The motor road's traffic and promotion manager was none other than the passenger railroad's most vigorous promoter, Sandford H. Cohen. In his typical fashion, employing alliteration to its fullest, Cohen frequently promoted the motor road with the phrase "Making the Apex of Appalachia Accessible."

While construction of the Mt. Mitchell Motor Road required a large force of workers, the size of their job was small when compared with the building of the logging railroad. In just a few months the tracks of the railroad were taken up, the grade realigned in some locations, and the entire length surfaced with cinders. The motor road was dedicated on June 26, 1922, and a group of more than 200 newspapermen, railroad officials, and invited guests comprised the first party to make the ascent to Camp Alice by way of the road. So enthusiastic was a newspaperman from Columbia, South Carolina, that he wrote: "Half of the people of Carolina go to the North Carolina mountains to spend the summer, and I believe when I go back and tell my story about the trip to Mt. Mitchell, I will come as near depopulating the state as Colonel Cohen has the English language of its adjectives."

The Mt. Mitchell Motor Road quickly achieved the popularity of the passenger railroad. In 1923 nearly 13,000 people followed the

In 1922 the Mt. Mitchell Motor Road opened to enable visitors traveling by automobile to reach Camp Alice by way of the old Perley and Crockett Railroad grade. Photograph from picture postcard (ca. 1925) in North Carolina Collection, Pack Memorial Public Library.

nineteen-mile road to Camp Alice. On the Fourth of July alone, 800 visitors ascended the mountain. Because of the motor road, Mt. Mitchell continued to gain a national reputation. Approximately 55 percent of the people who utilized the road in 1923 were out-of-state visitors, with South Carolina, Florida, and Georgia supplying the greatest numbers. Two thirds of the states were represented, as were thirteen foreign countries. Virtually all of the visitation at this time occurred from June through October.

Because the road was wide enough only for one-way traffic, special regulations were required: automobiles were allowed to begin their ascent only between the hours of 8:00 A.M. and 1:00 P.M., and they were required to start down the mountain between 3:30 P.M. and 5:30 P.M. Persons remaining on the mountain overnight were obliged to plan their descents so that they would arrive at the lower terminus of the road prior to 7:30 A.M. The cost of the trip was $1.00 per adult, 50 cents for children between the ages of five and twelve, and no charge for children under five. In the mid-1920s about two thirds of those utilizing the road came in private vehicles and one third came in "public-service vehicles" (taxis). Ascending the motor road to Camp Alice could be done in half the time it had taken to traverse the route on the passenger train a few years earlier. Visitors could now make the entire thirty-five-mile trip from Asheville to Mt.

By the late 1920s Camp Alice had become considerably improved and expanded, making it the largest overnight accommodation ever located in the Black Mountains. Photograph (ca. 1930) supplied by the author.

Mitchell in a mere two hours. The age of rapid transportation had arrived in the Black Mountains.

Camp Alice was hastily expanded to accommodate the increasing numbers of tourists ascending the mountain. By 1924 the camp consisted of at least three large structures: the dining room, which had been improved; an "amusement hall" with a large fireplace; and a building that afforded overnight accommodations. Until the late 1930s, Camp Alice consistently provided simple food and comforts to the thousands of visitors who journeyed to Mt. Mitchell each season.

As if not to be outdone by Buncombe County inhabitants, Ewart Wilson, grandson of Big Tom Wilson, decided to construct a motor toll road along one of the logging railroad grades on the Cane River (Yancey County) side of the Black Mountains. Employing two or three dozen other residents of Yancey County, Wilson completed the road in 1925 and named it in memory of the most famous inhabitant of the upper Cane River valley, Big Tom. The toll road began two miles south of Pensacola and continued for eleven miles to Stepp's Gap. From the gap to within a quarter-mile of Mt. Mitchell's summit, two miles of road were surveyed and constructed along the ridgeline of the Black Mountains, a route followed at the present time by N.C. Highway 128. A short connector road led from the Big Tom Wilson

101

Motor Road at Stepp's Gap to the Mt. Mitchell Motor Road at Camp Alice. By utilizing both of the toll roads, visitors could make a pleasant loop trip across the Black Mountains by passing through the towns of Asheville, Black Mountain, Burnsville, and Mars Hill. The Big Tom Wilson Motor Road had a steeper grade (7½ percent) and was somewhat rougher than the Mt. Mitchell Motor Road, and these factors, combined with a relative lack of tourism and poorer road conditions in Yancey County, resulted in the Yancey road's receiving less use than the one in Buncombe.

Not everyone who ascended Mt. Mitchell availed himself of the two toll roads. Hundreds of persons annually continued to climb the mountain by way of several trails, convinced that their extra efforts brought them added rewards. Most day hikers traveled on foot, but many campers took packhorses or mules to carry tents, blankets, and other camp items. With the city of Asheville's acquisition in 1903 of the drainage of the North Fork of the Swannanoa River as a watershed, use of the old trail past the remains of the Mountain House was prohibited. A new trail from the Swannanoa valley to Mt. Mitchell was constructed in 1903 to take its place. Beginning in Montreat, the trail wound to the high peak by way of Graybeard, Blue Ridge Pinnacle, and Potato Knob. Many of the hikers who utilized this trail came from the major religious assemblies that had recently been established in the upper Swannanoa valley.[29] To the east of the Blue Ridge, a twelve-mile trail was constructed from Graphiteville to Mt. Mitchell about 1915.

Meanwhile, on the Yancey County side of the Black Mountains, the trail from the Cane River valley up Big Spruce Pine Mountain to Mt. Mitchell went out of use as private interests acquired the hunting and fishing rights to the 13,000-acre tract at the headwaters of the river. As if to make up for the loss of the trail, both the United States Forest Service and Mt. Mitchell State Park included trail-making in some of their earliest work projects; by 1920 the Forest Service had constructed a trail from the South Toe valley near Busick to the summit of Mt. Mitchell and the state park had built a trail along the Black Mountain crest from Mt. Mitchell to Cattail Peak.

Visitors who reached the summit of Mt. Mitchell, whether by hiking or utilizing the motor roads, found a new, more solid observation tower that was constructed from native stone. Two years in the building, the tower was completed in 1926 at a cost of approximately $25,000. Such an expense was impossible for the meager state park budget to handle at that time, but the cost of erecting the structure was magnanimously donated by a private citizen, Colonel Charles J. Harris of Dillsboro, North Carolina. In June, 1927, the tower was officially dedicated "for the benefit of the people of the State and the permanent protection of the forests of the region."

102

A new stone observation tower was completed on the summit of Mt. Mitchell in 1926. Photograph (ca. 1930) from picture postcard in North Carolina Collection, Pack Memorial Public Library; supplied by the author.

During the early decades at the state park, the duties of rangers were less oriented toward recreation than they are at the present time. Indeed, it appears that until the middle part of the century, the two primary duties of rangers stationed at Mt. Mitchell were to watch for forest fires and to record weather data. During the spring and autumn fire seasons, watching for fires throughout the surrounding area was unquestionably the most important duty of the Mt. Mitchell rangers. This responsibility was later assumed by the United States Forest Service and the North Carolina Forest Service. Weather observations were taken sporadically at Mt. Mitchell from 1922 until 1936, when the peak was designated an official United States Weather Bureau station. At that time, the park's single ranger was given an assistant, whose primary responsibility was to make nighttime observations. Mt. Mitchell served as an official recording station for two decades, after which time a greatly increased number of visitors to the park usurped the attention of a growing ranger staff.

During the early twentieth century, improved transportation in the South Toe valley led to its decreasing isolation. This in turn permitted it to become an important destination for the rapidly expanding recreation-seeking public. By the mid-1930s Carolina Hemlock Campground had been established along the South Toe River and was attracting 15,000 campers a season. The 50-acre campground offered both tent and trailer camping, picnicking, and such recreational activities as swimming, horseshoe pitching, and hiking. Not

103

only did long-distance trails into the Black Mountains beckon the hiker, but shorter nature trails within the campground were made available for those who desired to learn about nature at an easier pace. The campground even had a council ring—a forerunner of the amphitheater—for such activities as community singing or marshmallow roasting around a campfire.

Until the 1930s Mt. Mitchell State Park was essentially lacking in facilities for public use. Between 1936 and 1941, however, Camp SP-2 of the Civilian Conservation Corps helped to remedy that situation. This CCC camp was no small operation, consisting of thirty-six buildings located about one mile south of Mt. Mitchell's summit. Perhaps the major accomplishment of the one hundred to two hundred workers was the construction of a facility still in use at the present time: a large, wooden refreshment stand and rest room complex located just below the summit. The CCC also constructed a pumping reservoir at Camp Alice and laid a pipeline from there to the summit area. In addition, it accomplished considerable trail work and fire-hazard reduction.

The CCC at Mt. Mitchell prepared the state park for the increased use that was anticipated with the completion of the proposed Blue Ridge Parkway, a roadway that represented a new idea in modern recreation. This 477-mile road, designed for recreation and pleasure, was first envisioned in 1909, but it was not until about 1930 that the construction of national parkways was being considered in earnest. Several short historical parkways were built in Virginia during this period, and in 1933 the first parkway to emphasize natural beauty was proposed. It was to be a so-called "park-to-park highway," connecting Shenandoah National Park in Virginia with Great Smoky Mountains National Park in North Carolina and Tennessee. Recreational travel was the single greatest use of highways at that time, and construction of a parkway would serve both to meet that need and to help ease the Great Depression by employing several thousand men for at least two years. Although several individuals wanted the road eventually to pay for itself, North Carolina insisted that it be made toll free.

While the decision to build a parkway between the two national parks was made with relative ease, determining the route of the proposed roadway provoked a great deal of lobbying, politicking, and controversy. Because of the anticipated benefits the proposed parkway would bring to the tourism industry along its route, Virginia, North Carolina, and Tennessee vied to obtain as much of it as possible. Each state was asked to propose its own route. In June, 1934, an advisory committee appointed by Secretary of the Interior Harold L. Ickes recommended that the southern half of the road be split evenly between North Carolina and Tennessee, but in November Secretary Ickes made the decision to route the parkway solely through Virginia and North Carolina. Ickes's decision was significantly influenced by his belief that the higher-elevation routing proposed by North Carolina offered a greater scenic advantage. Ickes was also swayed by the considerable political influence of Josephus Daniels, a North Carolina native who had acquired the post of United States ambassador to Mexico.

In 1935 construction of the Blue Ridge Parkway began in sections, the priority of which depended upon the anticipated recreational benefits and unemployment relief to be gained. By 1939 the section between N.C. Highway 80 and Black Mountain Gap had been completed. The following year, North Carolina evidenced its strong desire to keep all its roads toll free by taking over, widening, and improving the 6½ miles of toll road from the Blue Ridge Parkway dead end at Black Mountain Gap to the terminus of the old Big Tom Wilson Motor Road near the summit of Mt. Mitchell. For the first time, visitors had a toll-free means of access to Mt. Mitchell by way of a motor road. With the opening of this toll-free road and the soon-to-be-completed Blue Ridge Parkway to Asheville, the operation of the remaining toll portions of the Big Tom Wilson Motor Road and the Mt. Mitchell Motor Road soon became economically unfeasible, and their deterioration ensued.

The road from the Blue Ridge Parkway to Mt. Mitchell via Camp Alice was intended to be used only for a brief time. A new, shorter road—present-day N.C. Highway 128—had been proposed by the North Carolina Highway Commission with the strong backing of Governor J. Melville Broughton. World War II, however, prevented the road from being built until the 1946 and 1947 construction seasons. In 1948 visitors to western North Carolina could travel almost to the very summit of Mt. Mitchell by modern, two-lane paved highways. Two years later the Blue Ridge Parkway was opened from Black Mountain Gap to the vicinity of Asheville. This latter extension of the parkway reduced the traveling time from Asheville to Mt. Mitchell to approximately one hour. The result was that during the 1950 tourist season, visitation increased dramatically and, for the first time, more than 200,000 people entered Mt. Mitchell State Park.

The presence of the Blue Ridge Parkway and N.C. Highway 128 caused the development of visitor facilities in the vicinity of Mt. Mitchell to gravitate from Camp Alice to the ridgeline of the Black Mountains. By 1948 the current picnic area and small tent camping area had been established, the former near the summit of the high peak and the latter about halfway between Stepp's Gap and its summit. Atop Mt. Mitchell, the present parking lot was built in a

By 1939 the Blue Ridge Parkway had been completed between N.C. Highway 80 and Black Mountain Gap, just southeast of Potato Knob. By 1950 the completion of the parkway around the southern end of the Black Mountains to Asheville and the completion of N.C. Highway 128 to Mt. Mitchell's summit dramatically increased visitation to Mt. Mitchell State Park. Photograph from *State*, XVI (July 17, 1948), p. 1.

relatively flat meadow, presumably the same small glade through which Elisha Mitchell had passed in 1835. Then, in the early 1950s, a $240,000 capital improvement program authorized by the 1947 and 1949 state legislatures resulted in the construction of the present restaurant and lounge building, a park museum, and an enlarged summit parking lot. As a capstone to these developments, the present modernistic, concrete observation tower was erected on Mt. Mitchell's summit in 1959 and 1960 to provide a safer stairwell and larger observation deck than those available in the 1926 tower.

During the quarter-century of state park development from 1935 to 1960, almost every relatively flat location between Stepp's Gap and Mt. Mitchell became occupied by a building or two. One should not assume, however, that the state of North Carolina sought uncontrolled development for its first state park. A 1937 master plan for the park indicated that a desire to protect the natural environment also existed. This desire was expressed in decisions to permit no facilities other than foot trails north of Mt. Mitchell and to limit the size of the camping area to about twelve tent sites. Nevertheless, a number of

106

The present modernistic observation tower on the summit of Mt. Mitchell was completed in 1960, replacing the more somber stone structure that had dominated the high peak since 1926. Photograph (ca. 1964) courtesy Travel and Tourism Division, North Carolina Department of Natural Resources and Community Development.

individuals felt that too much development was occurring in the state park. Their voices, however, appear to have been neither loud nor organized.

Not all development near Mt. Mitchell was deemed suitable by state park officials—the private facilities in Stepp's Gap being the most notable example. This development, which followed the opening of the Big Tom Wilson Motor Road, was built and managed by Ewart Wilson and other Wilson family members. Over the years it gradually increased in size, and by 1960 "Camp Wilson" comprised a half-dozen enterprises: 2 gasoline stations, 2 souvenir shops, a cafe, and a small two-story inn. While many motorists no doubt appreciated the Wilson facilities, officials of the state park system considered them an eyesore that was particularly troublesome since it was located at the motor entrance to the state park. Because of the park's policy forbidding hunting within its boundaries, park officials undoubtedly also objected to the large pack of bear hounds that were kept at the development. For at least two decades, state park officials attempted unsuccessfully to acquire the Wilson land at Stepp's Gap, but it was not until 1962 that Ewart Wilson lost the battle to keep his land from becoming part of the state park. Camp Wilson was soon dismantled.

Ironically, at the same time that state park officials sought to acquire the Wilson family's inn and other facilities in Stepp's Gap, they were seeking approval for their own enterprise, to be known as

107

Mt. Mitchell Inn, one mile further up the road. This facility, projected to be built in the early 1950s at a cost of $133,000, became the most recent in a series of unsuccessful twentieth-century attempts to build a lodge atop the ridgeline of the Black Mountains. Much earlier in the century, the construction of the Mt. Mitchell Railroad had spurred several propositions to build a hotel atop Mt. Mitchell. For example, in 1916 a group of businessmen proposed building a modern, fifty-room hotel, complete with electric lights and private baths in every room. But while the plans of private developers in the early 1900s do not seem to have proceeded much beyond the minds of the men who proposed them, the attempt by the state to erect a lodge in the early 1950s almost materialized. Only when it was discovered that the funds allotted for the facility were insufficient did state park officials decide that, rather than going back to the state legislature to ask for more funds, they would scrap the lodge and instead construct a restaurant and lounge building.

A downhill ski slope and a new road to the high peak are examples of additional developments that have been proposed for the Mt. Mitchell area within the past few decades. During the 1950s, when downhill skiing was first introduced to the higher slopes of the southern Appalachians, the Mt. Mitchell area did not escape the attention of those interested in the sport. To promote their interests, citizens from Asheville and Charlotte formed the Mt. Mitchell Ski Club during the summer of 1956; and the following winter, with the permission of state park personnel, the club cleared and utilized a 700-foot by 150-foot experimental skiing area on the slopes of Mt. Mitchell. Both the Asheville Chamber of Commerce and the *Asheville Citizen* endorsed the development of skiing at Mt. Mitchell; but state park officials were concerned about the soil erosion that a ski slope would cause, and they refused to adapt any of their facilities to accommodate this or any other type of wintertime activity. Also in conflict with the promoters of skiing was the desire among Blue Ridge Parkway authorities to keep portions of the parkway closed during the winter because of adverse road conditions. The opposition on the part of state and federal government officials held sway, and skiing at Mt. Mitchell did not progress beyond experimental operations.

In a considerably more recent proposal, advanced in 1982, the Black Mountain-Swannanoa Chamber of Commerce pushed for construction of a year-round road from the Swannanoa valley to Mt. Mitchell, both to promote the economy of the valley and to provide cross-country skiers access to the Black Mountains. Because of a lack of money for new construction, the proposal was denied by the North Carolina Department of Transportation. Authorities of that agency did, however, leave open the possibility of such a road at a later time and noted that they might also be willing to reestablish a railroad on the old Perley and Crockett railroad bed.

Another recent development—occurring in the late 1970s—had an even greater potential for changing the Mt. Mitchell area. This was a movement to make Mt. Mitchell the nucleus of a national park of 100,000 acres or more. Such a proposition was not new to the Mt. Mitchell area. In 1924 the area, along with other southern Appalachian locations, had been examined for national park suitability; two areas that eventually resulted from that study were the Great Smoky Mountains National Park and Shenandoah National Park. Later, in 1969, an Asheville businessman, John M. Reynolds, proposed that the Mt. Mitchell area be made a national park or national recreation area in order to provide additional recreational land in the region. Reynolds's proposal, which was motivated in part by overcrowded conditions he had experienced in the Great Smokies, failed because he was not able to elicit adequately the interest of others.

A 1976 proposal, however, gave every indication that it would be different. On September 14, 1976, Michael Frome,[30] one of America's foremost environmentalists, proposed in the *Asheville Citizen* that the Mt. Mitchell area be made a national park. Frome thought the park qualified for such designation on the basis of its scenic and wilderness resources (earlier that year the National Park Service had designated the park a national natural landmark), but he also felt that establishment of a national park would be a particularly appropriate tribute to Roy A. Taylor, a retiring congressman from the town of Black Mountain and longtime chairman of the House Subcommittee on National Parks and Recreation.

Frome's proposal set the wheels in motion. Just a few days later, Congressman Taylor amended an omnibus bill that pertained to new area studies by the National Park Service to include the Mt. Mitchell area. The land placed under study was approximately 240,000 acres in size, extending from U.S. Highway 19E on the north to U.S. 70 on the south and from eastern Buncombe County on the west to western Mitchell and McDowell counties on the east. Taylor's bill directed the secretary of the interior in consultation with the secretary of agriculture and the governor of North Carolina to submit to Congress a study of the feasibility and suitability of including the Mt. Mitchell area as part of the national park system. The bill precipitated no major controversy in Congress, and within two weeks of its introduction it had become law.

Neither Frome nor Taylor appears to have anticipated the resistance that was to be put forth by citizens of Yancey County, the county encompassing a majority of the roughly defined area placed under study. Although the size of this area had been established more

109

for informational purposes than for indicating the precise area to be included in the proposed national park, the large majority of the approximately 5,000 Yancey citizens residing in the area quickly voiced the desire that their homes and land not be taken for a park. Yancey citizens also expressed their disapproval of the proposed national park because such a designation would prohibit hunting; fuel gathering; and the collection of moss, shrubs, galax, and berries—activities in which they were permitted to participate on national forest land in the area. Some individuals—including those outside the study area—were also concerned that their quiet, rural way of life would be lost as a result of the increased visitation that a national park would bring to the region. The certainty of a tremendous increase in visitation can be seen in a comparison of current figures for Mt. Mitchell State Park and for Great Smoky Mountains National Park: the former currently receives about 300,000 visitors each year; the latter, more than 8 million visitors annually.

The citizens of Yancey County voiced their disapproval of the proposed national park both individually and through citizen-action groups. Moreover, the likely supporters of the national park—developers and environmental groups concentrated in Buncombe County—appear either to have been apathetic or undecided as to their position. The *Asheville Citizen* and the *Hendersonville News-Times* expressed their support for establishment of a national park, but the citizens of western North Carolina appear to have lacked the will or desire to counteract the strong views of a majority of Yancey residents. The end result was that the movement failed. In mid-1977 Representative Lamar Gudger, who replaced Roy Taylor in the House, publicly expressed his opposition to the formation of a national park. In 1978 the state of North Carolina dealt the proposition a major blow by issuing a statement declaring that it was "unalterably opposed" to giving up its first state park. The intergovernmental study group that had been formed to investigate the suitability and feasibility of a national park produced six management alternatives[31] for the area but made no specific recommendation. In light of the forceful local and state opposition to changing the status quo, it is not surprising that the Department of the Interior dropped its consideration of Mt. Mitchell for national park status in March, 1979.

The movement to establish a national park at Mt. Mitchell, though unsuccessful, raises important questions for the future. What level of visitation can the Mt. Mitchell area accommodate without irreversible or excessive damage to the environment? What level of development is most appropriate for the area? What type of policy is most suitable for the management of the government land in the area—the multiple-use policy of the United States Forest Service or a policy emphasizing preservation and recreation, such as that followed by the North Carolina and national park systems? What is the likelihood of an increasing degree of retirement and second-home development, including such large-scale real estate enterprises as Mt. Mitchell Lands, which comes complete with a golf course? Should controls be placed on the thousands of acres of private land on the slopes of the Black Mountains? Can the current mix of private and government land be improved upon? How can the beauty and significance of the range be best preserved for future generations?

The Mt. Mitchell area has changed a great deal since the first settlers and scientists entered it two centuries ago. From the mid-1800s on, various developments related to tourism periodically arose and declined. Environmental change reached a crescendo during the timber exploitation of the early 1900s. At the present time the Mt. Mitchell area not only faces the potential threats of increased development and overuse but also contends with man-induced biological and chemical threats in the form of the balsam wooly aphid and acid

One of the most recent environmental threats to the Black Mountains is the destruction of balsam trees by an insect known as the balsam woolly aphid. In addition to forest damage caused by the balsam woolly aphid and windfalls, some scientists believe that atmospheric pollution is involved in the mortality of high-elevation trees. In this view from Mt. Gibbes looking north, damage to balsam trees, probably from balsam woolly aphids, is visible in the foreground. Photograph (1975) by the author.

111

rain. The aphid, a non-native insect with no natural enemies, appeared in the southern Appalachians in the 1950s, almost certainly as a result of man's activities. And acid rain, a problem only recently identified in the Mt. Mitchell area, results from man-induced atmospheric pollution whose source may be hundreds of miles away. The significant degree of cloud cover at higher southern Appalachian elevations causes the deposition of acid chemicals in the high-mountain soil; the chemicals in turn are believed to prevent or greatly inhibit the growth of trees and seedlings.

Thus, the very forest that Locke Craig thought he had preserved in 1915 is once again under attack. The long-term results of these threats are currently uncertain, but environmental change appears inevitable. The human and environmental history of Mt. Mitchell and the Black Mountains continues to be written.

Notes

[1]Thomsonians, or untrained doctors, flourished on the American frontier in the early 1800s. They were also called Indian doctors, botanic physicians, and quacks, depending upon who was describing them. One of the most famous practitioners was Samuel Thomson (1769-1843), for whom the occupation was named.

[2]Samuel Botsford Buckley (1809-1883) was an American botanist and geologist active in various portions of the eastern United States.

[3]Lewis Reeve Gibbes (1810-1894) was a professor of mathematics and physical sciences at the College of Charleston, Charleston, South Carolina, from 1838 to 1892. By interest, he was also a botanist; and although he held an M.D. degree, he was never a practicing physician.

[4]A trigonometric survey is performed by establishing a hypothetical series of triangles over the landscape. At each vertex, a triangulation station is established, and the horizontal angles between it and surrounding stations are measured in order to determine the position of and distances between the various stations.

[5]A water level could be one of two types: two glass cylinders connected by a tube and filled with water, from which a horizontal plane was determined when the level of water in each cylinder was at an equal height; or a sealed glass tube containing water and an air bubble, from which a horizontal plane was determined when the bubble reached a designated position on the instrument. Either type of level could be used to determine which peaks were above or below that upon which a person stood.

[6]The Green Ponds, probably two of them, were located near the confluence of Sugarcamp Creek and Cane River. The ponds do not presently exist, and it is not known whether they were natural or man-made.

[7]This refers to that portion of the United States which had up to that time achieved statehood.

[8]As used here, "Confederacy" refers not only to the southern states but to the entire United States.

[9]LeConte (1823-1901) was a professor of geology at the University of South Carolina at the time he performed his work in the Great Smoky Mountains. He later moved to California, where he engaged in notable work in the earth sciences.

[10]Emmons (1799-1863) was a state geologist in North Carolina during the mid-1800s. In 1853 he became embroiled in a dispute with Elisha Mitchell over the extent and value of the state's Deep River coalfields.

[11]In 1858 Clingman advanced his belief that a peak of the Great Smoky Mountains (Clingman's Dome) was higher than any in the Black Mountains. Although there ensued the question of which western North Carolina peak was the highest, Mitchell was not involved; he had died during the previous year.

113

[12]Silliman (1779-1864), professor of chemistry and natural history at Yale University for more than fifty years, was the founder of the *American Journal of Science and Arts*, probably America's foremost scientific journal of the nineteenth century.

[13]Henry (1797-1878), a nationally prominent physicist, was the first secretary and director of the Smithsonian Institution; he served in that capacity for about thirty years.

[14]Clingman believed that Mitchell's 1844 measurement of 6,672 feet had been taken on present-day Clingman's Peak. The congressman added 60 feet to Mitchell's measurement because a recent railroad survey caused him to estimate the elevation of Asheville to be 60 feet higher than the figure Mitchell had assigned to it in 1844.

[15]Such a conclusion was derived from Mitchell's 1835 statement that the high peak lay between the "North and Middle forks of Caney River" and Clingman's belief that the North Fork was the same watercourse as the Cattail Fork.

[16]How much effect the evidence of Mitchell's proponents had on Clingman's discontinuation of the controversy is not known. Clingman's newfound interest in the Great Smoky Mountains and Mitchell's death and burial on the high peak also were likely involved.

[17]Agassiz (1807-1873) was a prominent Swiss-American scientist noted for his studies on the classification of animals, especially fossil forms, and on the movement and distribution of glaciers. He immigrated to the United States in 1846 and two years later became professor of natural history at Harvard University.

[18]Black Dome is the name Guyot gave to present-day Mt. Mitchell. The name failed to come into popular use.

[19]The peak Guyot called Black Brother is presently known as Balsam Cone.

[20]The second-highest peak of the Great Smoky Mountains is named for Guyot. In addition, peaks in New Hampshire and California, both named Mt. Guyot, honor the professor's work in those states.

[21]Davis (b. 1901) has served as a professor of botany at various universities in the South. In contrast to his work in the Black Mountains, he later specialized in tropical and subtropical flora.

[22]Among those species whose numbers were greatly reduced and in some cases extirpated in the nineteenth and early twentieth centuries were the timber wolf, the mountain lion, the golden eagle, the bald eagle, the peregrine falcon, Bachman's sparrow, and Bewick's wren.

[23]Mitchell County, which was established east of Yancey County in 1861, developed into North Carolina's primary mining county. Its name appears to have been proposed or strongly promoted by the same people who supported Elisha Mitchell during the Clingman-Mitchell controversy.

[24]The town of Black Mountain, named for the range rising to its north, was incorporated in 1893. Prior to incorporation, it was known as Grey Eagle.

[25]The Clinchfield Railroad was at that time called the South and Western Railway. In 1913 it purchased the Black Mountain Railroad from the Holston Corporation and retained the Black Mountain road's name.

[26]The Mitchell Peak Park Commission, appointed on March 31, 1915, consisted of T. Edgar Blackstock of Asheville, chairman; G. P. Deyton of Green Mountain; D. F. Watson of Burnsville; M. C. Honeycutt of Burnsville; and Wilson Hensley of Bald Creek.

[27]Prior to 1947 the peaks presently known as Mt. Craig and Big Tom were called the Black Brothers because of their dark forest cover and their close proximity to one another.

[28]Asheville's population in 1916 was about 34,000, and the city reportedly attracted some 250,000 visitors annually.

[29]By 1916 the assembly grounds of the Southern Methodists, the Southern Baptists, the Presbyterians, and the YMCA and YWCA had all been established within four miles of the town of Black Mountain.

[30]Frome, a resident of Alexandria, Virginia, is the author of *Strangers in High Places: The Story of the Great Smoky Mountains* (Garden City, N.Y.: Doubleday, 1966; revised edition, Knoxville: University of Tennessee Press, 1980) and Rand McNally's *National Park Guide*.

[31]The alternatives were: (1) no change, (2) make the state park an extension of the Blue Ridge Parkway, (3) establish a national monument of approximately 15,000 acres in size, (4) establish a national park, (5) establish a national recreation area, or (6) establish a national preserve. Each of the latter three alternatives involved approximately 125,000 acres of land. The latter four options involved the acquisition of private land.

Research Sources and Suggested Readings

The large bulk of the research for this book was undertaken at the Sondley Reference Library of Pack Memorial Library in Asheville and at the North Carolina and Southern Historical collections of the University of North Carolina Library in Chapel Hill. All three repositories contain a wealth of material and are staffed by highly knowledgeable and helpful people. Other research help was provided by the North Carolina State Archives, the South Caroliniana Library of the University of South Carolina at Columbia, the Smithsonian Institution, the Library of Congress, the United States Geological Survey, the National Geodetic Survey, and the United States Board on Geographic Names. Letters, diaries, unpublished manuscripts, census and deed records, maps, newspapers, periodicals, and books from the eighteenth century to the present made up the large majority of the primary resource material that the author utilized. The following list of published sources includes some of the more significant and/or relatively accessible articles and volumes consulted:

"Among the Mountains of Western North Carolina." *Scribner's Monthly*, VII (March, 1874), 513-544.

Avery, Myron H., and Kenneth S. Boardman, eds. "Arnold Guyot's Notes on the Geography of the Mountain District of Western North Carolina." *North Carolina Historical Review*, XV (July, 1938), 251-318.

Battle, Kemp P. "Elisha Mitchell, D.D." *Journal of the Elisha Mitchell Scientific Society*, XXX (March, 1915), 157-164.

Blackmun, Ora. *Western North Carolina: Its Mountains and Its People to 1880*. Boone: Appalachian Consortium Press, 1977.

Burnett, Fred M. *This Was My Valley*. Charlotte: Heritage Printers, 1960.

[Clingman, Thomas L.] *Selections from the Speeches and Writings of Thomas L. Clingman*. Raleigh: John Nichols, 1877.

_____ . "Topography of Black Mountain." *Tenth Annual Report of the Smithsonian Institution* (1856), 299-305.

Colton, Henry E. *Mountain Scenery*. Raleigh: W. L. Pomeroy, 1859.

Deyton, Jason Basil. "The Toe River Valley to 1865." *North Carolina Historical Review*, XXIV (October, 1947), 423-466.

Frome, Michael. *Strangers in High Places: The Story of the Great Smoky Mountains*. Garden City, N.Y.: Doubleday, 1966; revised edition, Knoxville: University of Tennessee Press, 1980.

Guyot, Arnold. "On the Appalachian Mountain System." *American Journal of Science and Arts*, second series, XXXI (May, 1861), 157-187.

Hamel, Paul B., and Mary U. Chiltoskey. *Cherokee Plants and Their Uses—a 400 Year History*. Sylva: Herald Publishing Co., 1975.

Jolley, Harley. *The Blue Ridge Parkway*. Knoxville: University of Tennessee Press, 1969.

Lanman, Charles. *Letters from the Alleghany Mountains*. New York: George P. Putnam, 1849.

Memoir of the Rev. Elisha Mitchell, D.D., A. Chapel Hill: J. M. Henderson, 1858.

Michaux, Francois André. *Travels to the West of the Alleghany Mountains . . .* London: D. N. Shury for Crosby and Hughes, 1805.

Middleton, W. E. Knowles. *The History of the Barometer*. Baltimore: Johns Hopkins Press, 1964.

Mitchell, Elisha. "Notice of the Height of Mountains in North Carolina." *American Journal of Science and Arts*, XXXV (January, 1839), 377-380.

Mooney, James. *Historical Sketch of the Cherokee*. Chicago: Aldine Publishing Co., revised edition, 1975.

[Phillips, Charles]. "Dr. Mitchell's Investigations Among the Mountains of Yancey County." *North Carolina University Magazine*, VII (March, 1858), 293-318.

Pullman, Raymond. "Destroying Mt. Mitchell." *American Forestry*, XXI (February, 1915), 83-93.

Sargent, Charles Sprague, ed. "Journal of André Michaux, 1787-1796, with an Introduction and Notes." *Proceedings of the American Philosophical Society*, XXVI (1888), 1-145.

Savage, Henry, Jr. *Lost Heritage*. New York: William Morrow and Co., 1970.

Sondley, Foster Alexander. *A History of Buncombe County, North Carolina*. Asheville: Advocate Printing Co., 2 volumes, 1930.

Teacher Training Class of Burnsville. *History and Geography of Yancey County*. Burnsville: N.p., 1930.

"Timber Started Railroad Boom." *Yancey County Common Times*, December, 1976.

Van Noppen, Ina W., and John J. Van Noppen. *Western North Carolina Since the Civil War*. Boone: Appalachian Consortium Press, 1973.

Webb, Charles A. *Mount Mitchell and Dr. Elisha Mitchell*. Asheville: Asheville Citizen-Times Co., 1946.

"Winter in the South, A." *Harper's New Monthly Magazine*, XV (September, 1857), 433-451, (October, 1857), 594-606, (November, 1857), 721-730.